From the moment I b _____ *ki Hut, the Sharing of Life, Faith and Family,* I was drawn ... writing style is like having a conversation with a sweet friend. Her life and faith journey will give you hope, courage and trust in a God that loves the details of our lives. Grab some coffee or tea and a comfortable spot to read, because once you start this book, you can't put it down!

Liz DeFrain,
Women's Director,
PennDel Ministry Network.

Bev's book is absolutely wonderful! I appreciate her transparency and vulnerability to share some experiences from her life's journey that brought about faith and hope. Some stories will make you laugh, some cry. She enlightened my heart. It was beautiful to see the growth patterns of faith. She shares with such an openness—real life—exposing the heartaches, pain, joy and victories. These are stories that affect us all that we're sometimes very hesitant to talk about. I have always felt close to Bev and Jack, but after reading this book, I feel like I love them so much more.

Pastor Jim Rivera
Lead Pastor
City Limits Assembly of God

Bev and I have been friends for over 35 years. Her warm, heartfelt stories—many of which I remember —are a wonderful compilation of her faith journey. These have shaped her into who she is today—a woman who loves Jesus and hopes you do too. You won't be disappointed!

Jean Ross Harlan

TALKS UNDER THE TIKI HUT

The Sharing of Life, Faith, and Family

BEVERLY REINHARD FEKULA

WESTBOW
PRESS®
A DIVISION OF THOMAS NELSON
& ZONDERVAN

WestBow Press books may be ordered through booksellers or by contacting:

WestBow Press
A Division of Thomas Nelson & Zondervan
1663 Liberty Drive
Bloomington, IN 47403
www.westbowpress.com
844-714-3454

ISBN: 978-1-6642-5458-9 (sc)
ISBN: 978-1-6642-5459-6 (hc)
ISBN: 978-1-6642-5457-2 (e)

Library of Congress Control Number: 2022901797

Print information available on the last page.

WestBow Press rev. date: 01/28/2022

CONTENTS

DEDICATION

I dedicate this book to my husband, Jack. His support and love throughout our life together has been such a blessing. With every new adventure he has been right there offering his encouragement and support and—in the case of this book—his insight and editing skills. Thank you and love you, Jack! (Thanks for dancing with me!)

I also dedicate this book to my family and friends who over the years have created and continue to provide many precious stories.

ACKNOWLEDGEMENT

What creates great stories—a great cast of characters. Those characters have filled my childhood and my adult life with so many wonderful and wise life lessons that contributed to my faith journey.

I must thank my son, Joshua, who first introduced me to the Bible and Pastor Jim Rivera whose guidance, mentorship, and friendship, along with his wife, Deborah, have watered the seeds of my faith.

I so appreciate the blessings God has given me in all my children—Dennine, J. D., and Monica—I love their spouses as well—Paul, Teri and Jamie.

I always say that I love my children, but I'm "in love" with my grandchildren—Zachery, Julia, Michael, Sara, Jackie, Izzy, Genevieve, Sebastian and Nick (grandson-in-law to be). Then along came our first "great" grandchild, Kinsley. There are no descriptive words to express the love. What a joy at this stage of our lives! I say I'm a *great* grandmother—not bragging—just the facts! There are many more stories to be told by this family—either by me—or who knows who else will be inspired to author their own tales.

Thank you to all of the thirty plus people who have contributed to this book by sharing their joys and sorrows and to those who gave permission to reference or use their art images, give endorsements and encouragement.

And finally, I thank God for all the doors He opened for me that allowed my faith to grow over a lifetime. I know that there is more to come.

THE INSPIRATION

In Key Largo, Florida in our humble little community there is a small beach where the aqua blue ocean and the white, sun-bleached Adirondack chairs call to those who listen. Here, under the Tiki Hut, friends are made, acquaintances are renewed, and relationships are built. How? By sharing the stories of our lives.

Tug boat captains, attorneys, artists, musicians, pastors, realtors, doctors, widows, widowers, fisherman—the list is endless. We all have had interesting, some even fascinating lives. We all have stories and faith to share which creates a remarkable collage of experiences.

Any one of the short stories in this book could have, may have, been kindled by our talks under the Tiki Hut. As I wrote this book, I envisioned you and me sitting next to each other in those Adirondack chairs. During my life, I have had many experiences through my faith and family. As both have grown, I have learned to rely on God through the sunshine and the storms.

My prayer is that you feel the ocean breeze, delight in the sun and be encouraged by the God who made them and who inspired my stories.

THE BIRTH OF FAITH

Sometimes in the cool of the morning, I go to the Tiki Hut and find myself alone with God and my memories. I think of how I first encountered Him. As a little four-year-old girl, I remember occasionally seeing my mother cry. When I asked her why, she shared that she was missing her mother who had died many years before. She was still mourning her loss.

Death! Her mother died! Will my mother die? Will I die?!! I asked these questions although my young brain could not comprehend the answers—a time when my mother would not be alive—a time when I wouldn't be alive?

My mother shared about God and heaven and eternity. I still remember my brain almost exploding at the thought of forever...and ever...and ever...and ever—no end. As an adult, I still have trouble wrapping my brain around that thought.

But isn't this just the first time we consider faith in God? If I am going to spend forever...and ever—and ever, I want to spend it in heaven with a God who loves me. Of course, as we age and mature, faith grows just as we do—if we allow it.

My mother had a strong belief in God. I walked to church with her each week for Mass and watched her pray every night in her bedroom.

I saw her faith and she was definitely the first one to plant those seeds in me. I was the beneficiary of her faith.

My husband, Jack, and I recently traveled out-of-town to attend the funeral services of a friend's mother who lived to be ninety-seven years old. Although our friend is in her sixties and well educated, she asked me the following question with all the naivety and innocence of a child: "How long does it take to get to heaven?" I replied, "A lifetime." Seriously, the point is that no matter how old or educated we are, we still have those simple, childlike questions.

I would like to invite you to share my lifetime journey of faith. My faith is quite different today than it was as a young child. Different in what way? I can't simply answer that question in a sentence or two—hence, the book! Faith has been both a decision at a point in time and a process that is still growing and developing throughout my life.

I recently heard someone say that they didn't want to hear about faith from a twenty-year old, or thirty- or forty-year-old. They wanted to hear from someone older who had lived a full life—full of joys and triumphs, but also trials and heartaches. What difference can faith make in your life?

As a young girl, I was full of innocence and optimism. Life was going to be wonderful. Someday my prince would come, and life would be perfect.

Little did I know that my prince would not be an earthly man but a heavenly one who would guide, protect, and uphold me throughout my life.

I pray that God will open your heart and mind as you read these short stories. Faith is the substance they are written on. Some are serious, some funny, but all are real.

Now faith is the substance of things hoped for,
The evidence of things not seen.
Hebrews 11:1[1]

---

[1] All scriptural references in the book are from the New King James version.

A FORMATIVE EXPERIENCE

I was in third grade when my parents gave up their comfortable, rented home to move in with my grandparents. My grandfather had worked for the government in Harrisburg. My grandmother, now wheelchair-bound, was in need of care. My sister, Barbara Ann, was already married, had moved out and had a new baby boy.

My grandparents purchased a small, two-bedroom house in Emmaus, Pennsylvania and my parents offered to move in with them and help with my grandmother's care. My parents gave away all their furniture with the exception of their bedroom suite.

We all lived together for three challenging years. My grandmother had become quite cantankerous, frustrated, and very demanding. My mother worked in a factory from 7:00 a.m. to 4:00 p.m. and then came home to prepare dinner and care for my grandmother.

Looking back, this was a traumatic time for me as well—I was not allowed to bring any friends into the house, not allowed to speak to my mother while she was making dinner—I was truly not to be seen or heard! I felt quite invisible. I spent a lot of time outside riding my bike regardless of the weather.

It was definitely a difficult time for my mother who was very sweet and loving but very overworked and stressed. I'm not sure what the breaking point was, as I was only nine or ten years old. It must have been a heart-wrenching decision. From what I've heard, my mother was close to a nervous breakdown and the move was necessary for her health. My grandfather arranged for the needed health care for my grandmother. The day came when we moved out.

I can only imagine how humbling this must have been for my parents.

We moved into a two-bedroom apartment in center city Allentown—not in the best of neighborhoods. They had nothing but their bedroom set and a chaise lounge which had been my bed. We had a picnic table in the dining room, but here's the beauty—we were so happy! We had each other and loved each other—what more could we want?!

Life Lesson

In my adult life, this formative experience has had great impact and definitely influenced my values. Over the years, I have owned large, beautiful homes. I have also been a single mom living in a small two-bedroom apartment. Homes may come and homes may go, but the most important thing is the love that is shared within them.

> *Jesus says, "Take heed and beware of covetousness, for one's life does not consist in the abundance of the things he possesses."*
> Luke 12:15

BARBARA ANN

Up until now, I have not shared about my only sibling—Barbara Ann. She is thirteen years older than I am (a fact that I lovingly remind her of). When my mother became pregnant with me at the age of forty-two, my sister was appalled and embarrassed. She also saw no reason for another child as she was perfectly happy to be the only one. And she definitely didn't want to share her room with me.

She did influence my parents to name me Beverly Jean after a Southern beauty contestant winner she had read about in the newspaper. At least my namesake was a winner!

Looking back, I can see how I was a complete nuisance to her. When I was four years old, Barb was in high school. I became very ill with scarlet fever. The health department actually came to our house and nailed a quarantine notice on our front door. No one was to come or go from our home. My sister, who was anticipating the important social events of her senior high school year, had little sympathy for her ill little sister. She was allowed to leave and stay with a girlfriend until the quarantine was lifted.

I obviously survived. There were no antibiotics at that time and many children did die of the disease. I do vividly remember the sickness and isolation. My mother cared for me but from a distance. I recall extending my little arms out, inviting much needed hugs.

Another Barbara memory—when I was five years old, we still shared a bedroom, and she left her diary on top of our bed. She came into the room as I was paging through it. She yanked me by the arm and pulled me off the bed dislocating my forearm from the elbow socket. *Pain!* Mother quickly rushed me to Dr. Bausch whose office was just two doors away. One more purposeful yank and my arm was good as new.

As we retell this story, it's funnier now. A couple of years ago, this question occurred to me. I asked, "Barb, why were you so angry? I was five years old and couldn't even read yet?"

When Barb was nineteen years old, she married her high school sweetheart. I was her flower girl and I remember telling her she looked just like a princess. She and her husband were very prolific, producing five children. She was a great mother and was even featured on a full-page Mother's Day tribute in our local newspaper.

When I became older, married at nineteen and had my own children, our relationship evolved, and we became more like friends. She has always been there for me.

Now, when I drive her to her doctors' appointments, I remind her, "*This* is why you needed a little sister."

This year for her birthday, I decided to compose a poem rather than give her a Hallmark card. She loved it! I hope you do too.

I thank God for her.

Happy Birthday, Barbara Ann

I have a sister, her name is Barbara Ann
She gave me my name, Beverly Jean.
    Little could she see
    The Reinhard sisters we would be—
    Always.

Before I came along,
She was happy as a song
    The perfect *only* child she would be—
    Never.

She set the bar high.
It made me want to cry.
    The perfect "mother of the year" she would be.
    Sigh.

She was a great seamstress
Three prom gowns and a wedding dress—
    The prettiest one she would make for me.
    Surely.

She taught me to babysit.
It caused me a fit.
    But a mother myself I would be.
    Yeah.

When my life's dreams were shattered,
It caused her no matter.
    She said, "Come, live with me."
    Whew.

As we became older,
We grew closer and closer.
   A friend, a confidant, a great support
   She would always be to me.
   Blessed.

Grandchildren and "greats" we've gained,
But some things have always remained:
   The love that we share
   Because we are heirs
   Of the best parents ever!

Family love is forever.

Life Lesson

There's a saying that you can't choose your family. That's true—but you can choose to love them and encourage your relationships to grow. I was blessed with the family God chose for me.

> *Beloved, let us love one another,*
> *for love is of God;*
> *and everyone who loves*
> *is born of God and knows God.*
> 1 John 4:7

WHAT DO I BELIEVE?

It was Good Friday. I was at home with my two-year old daughter, Dennine. We were waiting for my parents to arrive as my mother wanted to take Dennine shopping for her Easter hat. This would only be the second year that Dennine benefited from our yearly traditional search for the perfect Easter hat. I had enjoyed this tradition for years and now I could see the tradition carry on.

My Mother was so in love with her youngest little granddaughter. It had taken six years for me to conceive and when I finally did, mother was ecstatic! She just loved to dote on her little angel. We anxiously waited for them. That's when the call came—"Your mother has suffered a heart attack and is in the hospital." No, that's not possible!

My Mother worked in a dress factory where the production line was quite intense and stressful. I had just asked her that week why she was working on Friday as she had recently retired. She replied, "They need me."

Evidently, the younger women could not keep up with the required pace of the assembly line and my mother became very agitated. She was not feeling well so they drove her home—home to my parents' third floor apartment. After trekking up the multiple flights of steps, she predictably felt worse, and my father called an ambulance to rush her to the hospital.

As we raced to the hospital, I was in complete denial. *(It's not a heart attack. She probably fell and just broke a bone.)* To my recollection, my mother had never been sick, never been in a hospital. She was a five-foot, four-inch bundle of energy and vitality. Always working, at the factory and at home.

She was so appreciative and impressed by the simplest things. Although my parents never owned a home, my mother decorated their apartment with minimal funds to look like *Better Homes and Gardens.* She was so talented and creative.

To me she was immortal—so strong and healthy! Surely, she would be with us forever. The fear of our own mortality began to take on a reality and gripped my heart.

Upon arriving at the emergency room, we found Mother sitting up in the hospital bed and complaining that she was starving because they hadn't fed her lunch. People who know me, will now think, *"That's* who Bev gets her appetite from!"

The doctors reported that my mother had experienced the mildest form of heart attack. There appeared to be little damage to her heart. However, they recommended that she be admitted and stay for three days for observation. Our local hospital had just launched a brand-new heart care unit complete with all the latest technology. We left feeling confident that she would receive the best of care.

The next day, Saturday, she was allowed two visitors at a time every six hours. My teenage niece had a great fear of hospitals so I offered to have her join me. As we entered the room, the first thing that caught my eye was a little picture of Dennine Scotch taped to the wall directly across from her bed. Mother was in great spirits and the visit was jovial and light-hearted. As we left, I turned back toward her, and our eyes met. That would be the last time I would see her. I always regret that I didn't have alone time with her. I wished I could have told her just one more time how great a mother she was and how much I loved her (and still do).

Early Sunday morning, Easter Sunday, about 4:00 a.m. my sister called and said that she heard from the hospital and Mother had taken a "turn for the worse." I still wonder if that's what they tell you to prepare you for the next message—the worst news you will ever receive. As I hurried to get dressed, the phone rang again—"don't come, Mother has died." My knees buckled as I dropped to the floor in shock and disbelief.

I had never lost someone I loved and to whom I was so close. The thought of never seeing her again, never hearing her voice, her laugh, her never seeing Dennine grow up. There would be no more Easter hats.

Waves of grief overcame me quite often. Like a tsunami, I would be overwhelmed with unexpected and sudden waves of grief. There really should be a better, more descriptive word than grief—it seems so weak and shallow. Even now, so many years later, as I write this, the tsunami returns to spill its tears and torment my soul.

The waves of grief would come back again and again over the years, but as time passed, the intervals between the visits would increase. I can say that the waves of grief subside but never cease.

I vaguely remember the viewing—so many people who knew and loved her. Many people with whom she worked thought that she was in her fifties. My mother never shared her age. As my sister and I met with the funeral director, he asked, "How old is your mother?" My sister and I looked shocked and wide-eyed turning toward each other, we simultaneously answered, "We can't tell you that—Mother would kill us!" It was the comic relief moment. Mother's tombstone bears only the date of her death.

My moment of truth came at the funeral Mass. It had been quite a while since I attended Mass. Was it really necessary?

Life Lesson

I remembered back when my mother was grieving her mother's death. When she had told me about God and heaven and eternity...forever and ever and ever...Where was she? Would I see her again? I know what she believed,

BUT WHAT DO I BELIEVE? It was a faith defining moment. Either I believed or I didn't. I chose to believe!

> *Jesus said to her [Martha],*
> *"I am the resurrection and the life.*
> *He who believes in Me, though he may die,*
> *He shall live.*
> *And whoever lives and believes in Me shall never die.*
> *Do you believe this?"*
> John 11:25-26

THE CHASE

Lou and I had been married for three years and were living in Liverpool, New York, just outside of Syracuse. We decided to go on our first vacation to Antigua in the British West Indies. I was very excited in anticipation of my first plane ride. Little did I know that the real excitement awaited me upon the return home.

Antigua was a beautiful island surrounded by an aqua blue ocean. It was quite undeveloped at that time. However, it did offer beautiful beaches and a luxury hotel complete with a casino.

Background

I met Lou on my first and only blind date—to a Beach Boys' concert. We dated for six months before we became engaged and married the following month. During those months, Lou was the perfect partner. Prince Charming. Very sweet and attentive. He went to church with me every Sunday, declined to go out with his friends even when I encouraged him, and he coached his little brother's Little League team. I envisioned him as a great husband and father. And, oh by the way, I *never* saw him gamble. That is . . . until the second night of our marriage, during our stay-at-home honeymoon, when our dining room was filled with his poker-playing, cigar-smoking friends!

Back to Antigua . . .

We had a relaxing visit except that Lou spent most of his time in the casino. Our plane ride home was uneventful as we flew into Philadelphia and then prepared to drive home to Liverpool.

I was driving on the Pennsylvania Turnpike and then Route 81 North. It was nighttime and the traffic was light. We approached the Syracuse exits and a little bit farther north I took the exit for Liverpool. That's when I noticed it—a black car parked right by the exit. I really didn't think too much of it—then it began to follow us. I turned right, he turned right. I turned left, he turned left. The pattern continued. I'm thinking, "Maybe it's just a coincidence." Reality quickly set in, and I yelled, "Lou, wake up. Someone is following us." The faster I went, the faster the black car went. This went on for about fifteen minutes. I was afraid to stop or to drive home.

We were in the quaint downtown village of Liverpool zigzagging in and out of little streets with the black car still in hot pursuit of us. Then it got worse. We saw their windows go down and drawn guns pointing directly at us. I drove as if our lives depended on it—because they did!

I pulled into the local police station at which point the pursuers changed direction and disappeared. We went into the station and explained what had happened. The police accompanied us home. I made sure they checked every room, every closet, under every bed to ensure no one was there. Of course, we still didn't feel safe and had a very fitful night's sleep.

Who were these men who so frightened us? I came to find out that when we left Antigua, Lou owed the casino a *considerable* amount of money. And the casino owners were not amused and quite upset. In a few days, I was told that "everything was taken care of." How? Lou had an uncle in Long Island, N. Y. who had "connections" and cleared up the whole matter. Who knew?

Life Lessons

In retrospect, I wish I had listened to my family who encouraged a long engagement. Anyone can be anyone for six months! One bad decision can affect the rest of your life. I stayed in the marriage for ten more years. I should have ended it sooner, but divorce was not in my family's vocabulary.

There are many more gambling-related stories—all sad and destructive. It was unfortunate. Lou was a very talented businessman, but his gambling addiction consumed him as well as our marriage.

As I look back to that stressful night in Liverpool, N. Y., I know that God gave me strength and protection as He continues to do until this day. Even as we experience the consequences of our bad decisions, He is always with us.

> *Fear not, for I am with you;*
> *Be not dismayed, for I am your God.*
> *I will strengthen you, Yes, I will help you,*
> *I will uphold you with My righteous right hand."*
> Isaiah 41:10

ON BEING A SINGLE MOM

N o one in my family had ever divorced. It was not an option.
I married at nineteen and after six years had a daughter, Dennine, and four years later a son, Joshua. I was very grateful that I was able to stay at home and nurture them. To me, it was the most important job in the world—the only job I every really yearned for.

I still worried about Lou and his gambling. I influenced him to attend a Gamblers Anonymous meeting in Philadelphia, but he didn't see the need for help. I accompanied him and attended the wives' meeting. What an eye opener! As the women went around the table and I listened to their experiences, I felt as if we were all married to the same man. I learned that with gambling, it really wasn't about winning or losing—it was about the high, the exhilaration. Like alcohol and drugs that high becomes addictive. After the meeting, the leader shared with me, "You'll know when you've had enough." It happened—I knew a few months later. After thirteen years in a tumultuous marriage, I reached my breaking point, packed up the two children, and left. Deep down, I was hoping that it might bring about a breaking point in Lou, which would incite him to get help and be the husband and father we so needed. This was not to be.

I was fortunate that my only sister, Barbara Ann, and her family welcomed us into her home. We set up a bed and crib in her basement and I promised to look for a job and an apartment and be out on my own in a month or two.

Yikes! "On my own!" What a scary thought. I had never lived on my own much less been responsible for two other human beings. I remember awaking in the middle of the night with such pangs of panic running through my whole body. I would pray for courage to God, whom I didn't really know very well and whom I felt was very far away. Little did I know that He was very close and guiding me.

I needed a plan—prioritize what I needed to do next. I literally had no money, no furniture and was driving a leased current-year Cadillac (which I knew I could not afford). First things first. I couldn't get a job without a car. Couldn't finance a car without a job. Couldn't buy a car without money. Again, I was enveloped with fear and panic.

What did I have? Jewelry! Fortunately, gold prices were high that year. I had my diamond engagement ring and several other valuable stones.

I enrolled Dennine in second grade at the local Catholic school and began searching for a day care for Josh. He was three years old and had always been with me. I tried out a nearby daycare, which was highly recommended, dropped him amid his tears and spent the morning visiting stores who might potentially purchase my jewelry treasures.

The bad news—when I returned to pick Josh up two hours later, he was still crying—the beginning of many guilt trip travels I would take.

The good news—sold all the jewelry I possessed and acquired one thousand dollars. Have you ever driven into a used car lot—driving a brand-new Cadillac—and inquired, "What do you have for one thousand dollars or less?" The salesmen thought I was either joking or crazy. I guess I was the latter.

After some scrupulous shopping, I learned the answer to my "one thousand dollars or less" question—*a 1974 Chevy Vega*. For those of you who are car enthusiasts, please stop laughing! I challenge you to go and sell all your jewelry and see what kind of a car you can buy for one thousand dollars cash!

Although affordable, it turned out that my Chevy Vega was costly to run—guzzling more oil than gas each week. However, it was a faithful vehicle for the time being.

Week one had been fruitful. Car found! Now the job search. I only had a high school diploma. I never had the desire to go to college. A nurse or a teacher seemed to be the only viable choices for females at that time. It didn't matter, as my parents did not have the means to send me to college. Our high school had an excellent business program which I completed and was hired as a secretary starting the day after high school graduation. That was great but now my resume was looking pretty bleak as I had not worked in seven years.

I began to research available jobs and submit my resume. My dream job was an interior decorator. A friend worked at the most exclusive and prestigious furniture store in our area at that time, Schoen's. Amazingly, they had an opening and she encouraged me to apply. I protested as I had no experience, but she persisted. The interview included creating a floor plan—which I had never done. More fear and panic!

I also applied to several local businesses, including Air Products and Chemicals, one of the best local employers at that time.

So, what happened? I received two job offers on the same day, one from Air Products and one from Schoen's. What a decision dilemma!

In comparing the choices, I really had no choice. Schoen's would require me to work Thursday nights and Saturdays. It would be difficult enough for the children to get accustomed to me working at all much less all those additional hours. Schoen's offered no medical benefits which were absolutely a requirement.

Air Products provided consistent eight-to-five work hours and excellent medical coverage. When I interviewed with Air Products, I quickly bonded with the Human Resource representative who was a recent widow with a daughter Dennine's age. She offered me a "coordinator" position. I accepted the position even before I knew what a coordinator was. I didn't realize that it was a level above secretary—a blessing for sure.

Next challenge—an apartment. I found a beautiful little apartment about a ten-minute ride from work and daycare. It even had a swimming pool.

My father blessed me with all sorts of needed kitchen appliances. We moved from my sister's in just five weeks from our arrival date—true to my word and thankful, ever so thankful.

As time went by and divorce was inevitable, a visitation schedule was developed so that the children could see their father every Wednesday night and every other weekend. Although it was difficult to be apart from them, I saw this as a positive as it provided structure and a regular schedule with more Dad time then they had when we all lived together.

When the children were away, there were times when I was lonely. I also had to ask myself what do I̲ like to do? I had always planned around everyone else desires.

I had no idea how full my life was to become. Air Products was definitely the right career choice.

Life Lesson

It is amazing to me how God directed me every step of the way. Even when we feel fear and panic, He does answer our prayers and provides courage and calm. I'm so thankful.

> *You enlarged my path under me,*
> *So my feet did not slip.*
> Psalms 18:36

A COLLEGE DEGREE?

I t was a wonderful experience to work for a large corporation. The pay was good, the people were great, the company was growing and there was so much to learn. However, I quickly realized how limited my future career growth opportunities would be without a college education.

For the first time in my life, I saw the advantage of a college degree. Fortunately, my company offered a tuition reimbursement program. As long as you earned a respectable grade, they would reimburse you for the tuition. There were two issues for me—first, I did not have the funds to pay for the tuition upfront along with the books, and a second, and even greater obstacle—lack of confidence. Did I possess the intelligence to pass a college course? I had not taken the college prep path in high school and was totally intimidated. What if I applied for the corporate program and flunked? Would they fire me?

My father provided great support and offered to loan me the upfront money for the course and books. Also, I decided that I needed to meet my fear head-on and try one class. To my utter amazement, I received an "A" grade.

For the first year or so, I took one class per semester. I tried to schedule classes that would coincide with the children's visitation schedule with their father. Sometimes, my father would come out and stay with the children.

Although I was pursuing the Business Administration/Management major, the school required that we take science and art classes.

The only course that truly challenged me was Chemistry. Yikes! I had not taken the college route in high school and had never had a Chemistry class. I must admit I was totally intimidated—and rightly so. I had no basic, fundamental knowledge. Most of the class participants were nursing students who had a solid background. I, on the other hand, felt as if I were in a foreign language class. I remember at breaks I would go for walks and cry! Another humbling experience! Eventually, I came up with a strategy—connect with those smart nursing students, join a study group, and read and reread the textbook. Miraculously, I passed with a "B" grade. My family still teases me. Every time the word "Chemistry" is mentioned, I shudder.

The most fun was the Ceramics art class. My expectation was that we would choose from shelves of pre-made ceramic items. For example, "I'll paint that little bunny on the top shelf." Oh no—we actually made the clay! I had volunteered to help with no idea what I was signing up for. The professor had these fifty-five-gallon drums into which we poured so many pounds of South Carolina clay and then more pounds of another type of clay. The professor then dragged out a long hose and added water to the mixture. The volunteers, including me, rolled up our jeans, took off our socks and sneakers and climbed into the drums where we did a little clay making dance. It reminded me of the *I Love Lucy* episode where she and Ethel made wine! It was definitely a memorable night—going home with dried clay all over my legs.

It was difficult working full-time and taking classes, but I used my lunch time and the quiet time after the children were in bed to study. Looking back, I so wonder how I managed.

Then it happened—*The Dance*! As you will see in the next chapter, God was about to bless me with the most amazing partner.

And the Lord God said,
"It is not good that man[2] should be alone;
I will make him a helper comparable to him."
Genesis 2:18

Life Lesson

Did I mention that I was thirty-three years old when I took that first college course? It took nine years, part-time, to earn a Bachelor's in Management from Cedar Crest College and three more years for my Master's in Educational Technology from Lehigh University. At that point, I was forty-five years old! That's when I was promoted to Global Learning Manager and began international travel. A perfect time in life—my children were in college or off on their own. Don't ever think you are too old. When someone tells me that they don't want to start their education because, for example, they would be fifty-years old when done. My response is "Yes, but you could be fifty-years old with a degree."

---

[2] or woman [my addition]

THE DANCE

I was settling in on being a single mom working at Air Products. The company anticipated the need for two hundred plus new positions that year as they were having a huge growth spurt. In my coordinator position, I was a liaison between Human Resources (HR) and the Information Technology (IT) Department.

Managers would specify the positions they needed. I'd inform HR who would invite potential candidates for interviews. My role would be to secure time with the appropriate four or five managers, enlist feedback and communicate our hiring intention to HR.

I got to meet so many new people. All the managers were super nice but also super busy. That's when I first met Jack. He was one of my "go to" managers who I could count on to make time for interviews. On occasion, we had the opportunity to talk at work and share a little bit of our lives and backgrounds. He also had two children, a boy and a girl. He seemed to be a real "hands-on" Dad. Once, unbeknownst to him, I saw him in the supermarket parking lot with his children. They were in the shopping cart laughing as he pushed them as fast as he could. They were having so much fun just being together. Jack and I became friends.

One night, there was a celebration for one of the IT employees and we were all invited to attend. It was held at a local bar/dance hall. I was extremely shy and nervous to attend alone and agreed to meet my girlfriend there. I was definitely NOT interested in dating or meeting anyone. I was happy to be on my own for the rest of my life.

It was fun to see so many people outside the work environment. Many people were dancing—I was observing. My girlfriend had to leave, and I was very self-conscious to be there alone. I had no experience being in this type of environment since I had married so young.

What happened next would be a forever, life-altering phenomenon! I should inform you that there are two different versions of what took place next.

First, I'll share Jack's version:

> I was just a wallflower. Were people dancing? Was I dancing? Really? Honestly, I don't remember that.

Now for my version—better known as the truth:

> I stood on the sidelines, and I suddenly noticed Jack on the dance floor. I watched for quite a while as he danced with *every single woman* in IT! Everyone but *me*!
>
> I felt totally demoralized. My self-esteem was already super low, and this felt like a significant rejection from my friend, Jack.
>
> What's a girl to do? Well, when his dance was over, I marched myself right up to him and exclaimed, "What's a girl got to do to get a dance with you?" I couldn't believe that those words were actually coming from my mouth.

That's when it happened—*The Dance*! The music began again with the song, *"Put Your Head on My Shoulder"* by the Letterman. We had no choice, we had to dance. And dance we did! It had been forever since a man had held me in his arms. I just melted.

In the future, Jack would share that he was totally SMITTEN! I'm not sure if there is such a thing as "love at first sight" but we are witnesses that there definitely is "love at first dance." We continued to dance the rest of the night until the music stopped.

This was the beginning . . .

I couldn't stop thinking about him. While all alone in my living room, I would pretend to still be dancing in his arms.

In his memory, he said that I had on a beautiful, white, flowing dress. In reality, I had on blue jeans and a pale blue blouse with a white collar.

This was the beginning of our story, our life together. We dated. Have you ever dated with six people—two adults and four children. We all got married on December 13, 1985. The children were ages eight, nine, ten and twelve. The children are all grown now with children of their own.

We still dance! Each year, we go out to celebrate our first dance. Today, our song is, *"Through the Years"* by Kenny Rodgers.

I thank God for Jack who really is the Prince Charming that I dreamed of as a little girl. He has stood by me and supported me in every aspiration—parenting, college, ministry, painting, and writing. He is the love of my life!

After Note

Ten years ago, I was diagnosed with Charcot-Marie-Tooth (CMT) disease, a neurological muscular disease that weakens the muscles in the legs and arms. The calves in my legs are quite atrophied which necessitate the wearing of leg braces.

We still dance! Now, Jack gracefully lifts me off the ground when he anticipates that I've lost my balance. I still melt in his arms, and he says that after all these years, he is still SMITTEN!

We thank God every day for bringing us together.

> *And now abide faith, hope, and love,*
> *These three;*
> *But the greatest of these is love.*
> 1 Corinthians 13:13

THE NOTEBOOK

During our first year of marriage, Jack and I had our hands full assimilating our two families. That year there was a teachers' strike and the usual Meet-the-Parents' Night was postponed until October.

Our oldest son, John David, nicknamed "J. D." was in the fourth grade. He was a shy, sweet, and smart little boy. We were anxious to meet his teacher and learn how his academic life was progressing.

As we entered the classroom, we were invited to sit in the children's chairs. Have you had this experience? Scrunching your tall, grown legs into a chair made for someone one third your size until your knees are almost touching your chin? Quite an exercise!

J. D.'s teacher, Mrs. Burnhauser, began her welcoming talk. It was the first time we met her, and to us, she appeared to step right out of a 1950's classroom—very prim and proper, professional, organized and very dedicated to teaching.

She updated us on her methods and communication procedures. She explained, "The nightly homework assignments, as you know, are in *"The Notebook."* All graded tests are in *"The Notebook."* If I sent you a personal note, it's in *"The Notebook."*

She went on and on and on about *"The Notebook."* With every statement, the other parents would nod and chuckle approvingly. There we sat totally perplexed and confused. Jack and I looked at each other and quietly whispered, "Do you know anything about *"The Notebook?"* To our dismay, neither of us had.

Finally, the session ended. We definitely needed to speak with her but were so mortified. We waited anxiously until every other parent left the classroom and finally had a chance to talk with her privately. With much embarrassment, we apologized and explained that we had no idea about *"The Notebook."* She was so kind and looked at us pitifully and said, "It's okay, Mr. and Mrs. Fekula, John told me that you couldn't afford to buy a notebook." *What*???—shock, disappointment, bewilderment but mostly anger began to arise—especially from Jack.

> An aside—Jack and I were both working professionals at a large corporation, making a more than decent living. *"The Notebook"* was nothing more than a three-ring plastic binder of which we probably had a dozen or more in our attic.

We asked to see J. D.'s desk. Its style was one that had a large opening of several inches right below the desktop. We peered inside and to our horror saw many, many papers crumbled into balls and stuffed inside.

One by one, we extracted the paper balls, smoothed the wrinkles out as best we could and eventually found every single paper that should have been filed in *"The Notebook."* We assured Mrs. Burnhauser that tomorrow, J. D. would arrive in her classroom with a notebook in hand.

Speechless, we walked out of the school and to our car. I don't know if I had ever seen Jack so angry.

And that's when the evening's title changed and became "The Night that Bev Saved J. D.'s Life!" I would not let Jack go right home. We drove around for an hour or so until Jack calmed down and composed himself.

When we did have a sit-down with J. D., it was very directive. His Dad was going to call Mrs. Burnhauser <u>every</u> weeknight to learn the homework assignment and it better be done! We gave him a notebook. That first year of our marriage, I think Jack spoke with Mrs. Burnhauser more than his new wife!

We did become friends with Mrs. Burnhauser and, along with J. D., visited with her and her husband. What a wonderful teacher and woman.

As I write this, I again wonder *why* J. D. initially ignored *"The Notebook."*

He had a lot of changes going on in his young life and perhaps that was one area he felt he could control.

In 1995, J. D. had just finished his freshman year at Penn State University. While attending his sister's high school graduation, guess who he happened to see? Yes, Mrs. Burnhauser! He had not seen her since fourth grade. Surprisingly, she remembered him. He was so very proud to tell her that he completed his first year at Penn State and had earned a 4.0 GPA!

After Note . . .

Today, J. D. is in his forties and Mrs. Burnhauser is in her eighties. They are "Friends" on Facebook—no notebook required.

Life Lesson

Raising children is a challenge—one that needs the wisdom of God. We must pray every day that He gives us patience and understanding.

> *Train up a child in the way he should go,*
> *And when he is old he will not depart from it.*
> Proverbs 22:6

AND IT WAS GOOD

I have always loved going to the beach. The ocean still captivates me. I am overcome by its massiveness. I feel closer to God as I remember how He created it all and how powerful He is. And it is still good!

I remember the very first beach vacation I had with my parents. They took me to Atlantic City's Steel Pier and we saw the diving horse. Yes, that was a real thing! I was a young child so I can't really recall the specifics of how it was done, but I do remember that there was this massive tank that the horse jumped into. For real! This was a big attraction at the time. Okay, I just Googled "Diving horse, Atlantic City Steel Pier" and there's a video! You can see it for yourself.

I still have a vivid memory of swimming in the ocean for the first time with my parents. My father and I were standing in the shallow waves watching my mother who was a little farther out but facing us. Unbeknownst to her, a huge, massive wave was racing up behind her. Bam! It crashed right into her, knocking her down, and pulling her under. Fortunately, she was a strong swimmer and recovered gracefully while my father and I laughed until our sides hurt.

Since my parents both worked during the day, I would spend my teenage summers at my sister Barbara Ann's house in the suburbs. My parents still lived in the two-bedroom, third floor apartment in the city, but by now it was fully furnished—no more picnic table in the dining room.

Barb is thirteen years older than I am. She was married at 19 and seemingly, to me, was always pregnant. I was the chief babysitter, a mother's helper of sorts. The highlight of the summer would be a two-week vacation to the beach at Wildwood Crest, N. J. Joe, my brother-in-law, would rent a U-Haul to attach to their station wagon to lug all the suitcases, beach toys and bikes for their family of five children plus me.

I was always thrilled when I was allowed to bring a girlfriend along. One afternoon my friend, Linda, and I were in the ocean. We were out about as far as previous days, but all of a sudden, we were caught in a rip tide which kept pulling us farther and farther out to sea. I remember yelling to Linda to stay on top of the water and keep swimming to shore. It didn't work. We were both flailing about and quite frightened.

I had learned about mortality with my Mother's death, and now I was facing my own.

Then, as if in a movie, our heroes arrived—a rowboat with two New Jersey lifeguards. We were rescued! It didn't take long for us to recover and realize, Wow! These guys are so handsome, tanned and muscular! This will be a great story to share with all our friends back home. They rowed us to shore where quite a group of spectators had gathered among whom was my sister—not at all amused or relieved—just angry. All I remember was her yelling at the top of her lungs (and with five children, she was quite proficient at that). "I brought you here to watch the children, how could I tell Mother and Daddy that you drowned"?! No one has forgotten this incident.

I believe that God had a greater purpose for my future and protected me that day.

Once I had my own children, I loved introducing them to the beach. When Dennine was just about a year and a half, we took her to the beach for the first time. I loved running down the beach with her and running right into the water and waves. It was so fun! When Josh came along, he too was a fan.

A few years later, when Jack and I married, our summer tradition was taking our four children to Long Beach Island (LBI), N. J. The boys, J. D. and Josh, had so much fun playing games in the sand. Monica loved the waves and could often be seen as the last person left in the ocean on a chilly day. These were simple, fun-filled days of fishing, crabbing, biking, playing jacks, visiting the amusement park and our favorite, the *Showplace*—which served ice cream and show tunes while engaging us in their theatrics.

Speaking of fishing—one day we rented a little rowboat with a small motor (we were on a tight budget). We promised the kids that we would take their pictures with the fish they caught. I packed peanut butter and jelly sandwiches for lunch and we set out on our ocean adventure. J. D. was great at casting—so great that on one of his first casts, he used so much force that he threw his whole rod, reel and all into the ocean! By some miracle, Jack was able to use his line and recover it.

Next, Monica decided that she needed to visit the rest room, resulting in our returning to the dock. Finally, we resume our fishing. It is now 10:00 a.m.—all the lunch sandwiches have been eaten. Josh gets a bite on his line and with much excitement pulls in—an *eel*! Yikes! As he pulls it into the boat, the eel falls off the hook and begins to slither about on the floor. Now everyone, but Josh, is screaming and scooting around. It's amazing that we did not capsize. Jack is not too thrilled with eels and tried to finesse it into a plastic garbage bag to dump it back into the ocean. Now Josh is crying because this is the fish he wants to take a picture with! Monica declares that she must again visit the rest room, resulting in another return to the dock.

While I'm waiting for her, I meet an old fisherman. I shared our eel experience with him, and he informs me that eels make great eating. They are a delicacy! Wow—who knew. That night, Jack and I attempted to clean the dead eel. According to the old fisherman, you just peel off the skin. We sure tried, but the eel was so slippery it was very difficult. Finally, we cleaned it and sautéed it. "Tastes just like chicken," said the old fisherman. Not true! We finally discarded that eel, but at least Josh did get his picture taken with it.

Josh with eel on right
J. D. with bluefish on left

J. D. and Monica with bluefish

Jack and I also have wonderful memories of romantic walks on the beach and dinners of French-fried lobster tail at Howard's Restaurant. (Still available to this day.) We recently visited LBI and had a sweet time reminiscing and missing those young children who are now grown and have their own children.

When my daughter Dennine and her husband, Paul, had their children, Julia, Michael, and Sara, I had the opportunity to share with them my love of running down the beach and into the waves.

When Sara was about five years old, we were at the beach, and I realized that due to my neuromuscular disease (Charcot-Marie-Tooth) I was no longer able to run down the beach and into the water. I thought about what I could still do that might be fun and memorable for her. I took her little hand and slowly led her to the sand at the edge of the water. We sat down and I asked Sara if she remembered how we made snow angels at home in the winter. She did. I explained that we were going to make sand angels! So, we both laid back in the sand, spread our arms and legs wide, and made sweeping angel-wing moves. We were laughing and enjoying ourselves until an enormous wave crashed about us leaving the water to recede and pull us into the ocean. With this, Sara put her little arms around my waist, held on to me with all her might and declared, "I got you, Nana, I got you . . . stay with me . . . stay with me, Nana." And I did. (One of my favorite Sara memories.)

Life Lesson

I am so thankful for all these memories. Thankful to our mighty Creator for the beauty He spoke into existence. Life is best experienced with family and faith in God.

> *And God called the dry land Earth,*
> *and the gathering together of the waters He called Seas.*
> *And God saw that it was good.*
> Genesis 1:10

THE LAST GIFT

J ack's mother, Lovdy, was a sweet, hardworking woman. Like my
mother, she worked in a dress factory for many years. She had had a
difficult life but still successfully raised two sons, Jack and David, and a
daughter, Penny. After her husband died, she lived in a tiny little house
on just $334 a month from Social Security. Still, she remembered each
of her children and grandchildren on their birthdays with a card, always
including a $5 bill as a gift.

The family was devastated when she was diagnosed with ovarian
cancer. She was adamant about staying in her own little home in
her comfy Lazy-Boy chair rather than going to a nursing home. Her
children honored her wishes by taking shifts so she would never be
alone. Hospice would also visit regularly.

One afternoon, Jack, Penny and I were sitting in Mom's living room
just casually talking with her. Soon the conversation turned to the topic
of my upcoming birthday—my fiftieth. Mom directed Penny to "get
the box." Like many of her generation, she kept envelopes in a little box
with designations for phone, electric, etc. Penny retrieved the box and
brought it to Mom who carefully and slowly walked her fingers through
the contents. Finally, she extracted a bill and asked Penny to give it to
me. I received it and looking at the amount I exclaimed, "Mom is this

right? Do you know that there's a zero at the end—*$50*?" Mom replied, "You're worth it." This still bring tears to my eyes.

Jack usually took the night shift watching her and then went to work. During the last night he spent with her, she called to him and woke him at 4:00 a.m. Jack quickly went to her and inquired if she needed to visit the bathroom. She replied, "Just hold me." As Jack helped her stand, she just stood still and held him tightly as they hugged. Then, she said, "Okay, you can put me down." I believe she longed for the warmth of her son's loving arms for one last time.

Mom passed away six hours later—in her chair, in her living room, surrounded by all her praying children and their spouses. What a sweet passing. I only hope I should be so blessed.

Life Lesson

Again, I was faced with the reality of our mortality. Mom's passing, with her children surrounding her was so different from my Mother's who passed on in the hospital without family—seemingly alone. I am reassured to know that she was not alone. Jesus, her Lord and Savior, to whom she prayed every day was there to be her comfort.

> *Yea, though I walk through the valley*
> *of the shadow of death,*
> *I will fear no evil;*
> *For You are with me;*
> *Your rod and Your staff,*
> *they comfort me.*
> Psalm 23:4

ANOTHER HUMBLING
EXPERIENCE

During my corporate business career, my company formed a joint venture with a German company. To celebrate the start of this partnership an extravagant luncheon was held. What was unique was that the luncheon was celebrated simultaneously in both locations— Trexlertown, Pa. and Munich, Germany. All of our top executives attended.

A video conference allowed us to see those at the other location and for them to see us. Modern technology! We just couldn't "pass the salt." Many round tables afforded us a comfortable atmosphere.

There were ice sculptures at both sites, fabulous food, and scrumptious desserts.

When the meal was finished, the festivities continued. It was announced that there would be a drawing. Under someone's chair was a tag that would designate them the winner. I'm not sure why but I was feeling particularly confident. It was time for the revelation!

I took my right hand and expectantly reached under my chair. Yes! I felt the tag. Now if I could just remove it. I had to tug a bit but off it came. "I have it! I got it! I got it! I won! "I won," I exclaimed in a loud voice heard around the world or at least in Trexlertown and Munich.

I looked down at the tag and to my chagrin realized that what I held was not the winning ticket but . . . the manufacturer's tag that read:

UNDER PENALTY OF LAW THIS TAG IS NOT TO BE REMOVED.

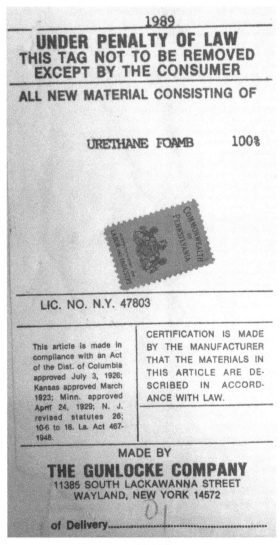

Furniture Tag

Another humbling experience. I had just made a fool of myself—GLOBALLY! Fortunately, the law did not show up and no arrests were made.

Life Lesson

I was recently asked if this experience would better be described as embarrassing rather than humbling. I believe that God uses <u>everything</u> in our lives. In this case, He used an embarrassing event to keep me humble. Now, when experiences like this occur (and they have), I simply laugh and reply, "Just another humbling experience."

> *Humble yourselves in the sight of the Lord,*
> *And He will lift you up.*
> James 4:10

CHESTER REINHARD

I've shared stories about my mother and sister in earlier *Tiki Hut* stories. Now I'd like to flash back so you meet my father, Chester Reinhard.

After World War II ended, my father returned from his security post in Bermuda, where they were building an airstrip. As my mother described it, the men returned home from World War II and many of their wives became pregnant—including my mother, who was forty-two years old! I was definitely a surprise to my parents and an embarrassment to my teenage sister.

There is so much I could write about my father, Chester Reinhard. He and my mother were very much in love. In my teen years, I remember coming home early from a date only to find my parents smooching on the sofa!

They had secretly married in the rectory of Sacred Heart Church since my father was Protestant and, at that time, not allowed to marry in the Catholic Church. Then my parents rented a house and threw a huge party for all their family and friends. (The marriage was to be a surprise!) They framed their marriage certificate, hung it on the wall, and waited to see who noticed it first—Grammy Reinhard. Quite an unusual wedding reception. I still have their framed marriage certificate along with their original bedroom set in our guest "Reinhard Room."

Marriage Certificate

"Chet" worked in various sales positions. I even have a picture of him selling Hoover vacuum cleaners door-to-door. Most of his career was spent at Sears and Roebuck fitting customers with custom-made suits.

He was very handsome—a Cary Grant type. Too young to know Cary Grant? Think George Clooney. Daddy even modeled as the groom in Hess Brothers Department Store's Wedding Show. (A very big deal back in the day.) I've been told that when my sister, who was only five at the time, noticed him on stage, she exclaimed, "That's my Daddy" much to the audience's delight.

During the time we lived with my grandparents, his job gave him a day off during the week. It was our "date" day. We always did something fun—miniature golf, pony rides and visits to amusement parks. He took me on my first roller coaster ride—insisting that we must sit in the very first seats to get a good view! And that we did! Could that be the reason I still avoid roller coasters to this day?

I could talk to him about anything. He always made sure I had a dime to call him[3] from a payphone[4] if I got into a bad situation. (I just can't imagine how we survived back then without cell phones!)

Life was not always idyllic. My father dealt with—we all dealt with—his alcohol addiction. You could call him a working alcoholic as he always kept his job. My mother's patience, prayers, and love for him sustained their marriage.

The day my mother died was his breaking point and sent him off the deep end. He was unable to face life sober. The doctors informed us that given his age and the recent death of his wife, Daddy had only a four percent chance of recovery and sobriety. This was devastating for our family as we felt we lost not only our mother but our father as well. After a family intervention, my father chose rehab. He was sober for the last seventeen years of his life. I was and am so proud of his recovery, influenced by his love of his family and his faith in God. Our family was so blessed.

Daddy just loved Jack. He would always say, "That Jack, he can do anything!" They would play golf together often. Jack could drive a golf ball a mile (my father loved to proudly watch) but when they got within one hundred yards of the hole, my father's "short game" always had Jack beat. Daddy played golf right up to the summer before he died at the age of eighty-seven. He would get out of the cart, address the ball, and very unsteadily take his swing. He would always connect with the ball—as if he were on auto pilot.

Daddy kept busy by working part-time at Leh's department store at the service desk. He was now into his eighties. The men's thrift section was right next to his security desk. One night, he noticed a young man loading up his arms with as much clothing as he could carry. The thief darted right past Daddy and out the side door to the alley. Does my father call the police? Oh no, he proceeds to chase the

---

[3] Yes, ten cents. You placed the coin into the phone and dialed your number.
[4] These large machines were usually on a street corner or outside a gas station.

shoplifter down the alley, yelling at him to drop the clothing—which surprisingly he did! From that time forward, he earned the nickname "Rambo Reinhard." Life was never dull.

I remember Daddy's last birthday. A family dinner was held at our house. For dessert, I made fresh fruit salad and of course, a birthday cake. As we all sang *Happy Birthday*, Daddy inhaled a deep breath and instead of exhaling air to extinguish the burning candles, he propelled a whole grape clear across the table as if it were a World War II bomb. We all laughed so hard. Evidently, he had forgotten to wear his dentures that day which might have helped contain the projectile.

We have so many wonderful memories of my father. I know that my mother spent much time each night offering prayers for the love of her life.

Life Lessons

Lesson One:
I believe girls receive their validation and their worth from their fathers. My father always affirmed me. I can recall several times in my young life when one of his male friends questioned him as to whether he was disappointed that I wasn't a boy. I would intently listen in on his answer. Daddy was always quick to respond, "Oh no, I love my girls." That meant so much to me.

Today, you hear a lot about how important a father's love and presence is in his sons' lives. Absolutely true! Equally true and important is the presence, love, and protection of a father in his daughters' lives. When the Bible says that God created them, "male and female He created them[5]". I believe it was not just to become parents, but to be parents—to play unique roles in their children's lives.

---

[5] Genesis 1:27

If you did not receive this parental presence in your life, please know that our Heavenly Father loves you and is always present.

<u>*Lesson Two:*</u>
It was such a heartache to watch Daddy in the throes of his addiction. God showed me that what <u>He</u> does matters, not what Doctors predict. God does not deal in odds or chances. I needed Daddy—our family needed Daddy as we would face future trials. I know it was Daddy's love for his family that gave him the faith and strength to recover and remain sober.

The past prayers of my mother and the prayers of our family were heard and answered.

> *For God is my witness . . .*
> *that without ceasing*
> *I make mention of you always in my prayers,*
> Romans 1:9

A SECOND CHANCE

Daddy was living alone in a beautiful high-rise for the elderly when he had a very strange experience. While he got up to visit the bathroom in the middle of the night, he felt very weak and passed out on the floor next to his bed. Sometime later, he managed to get himself back in bed. He knew he was in trouble. There was an emergency button on the wall over his head. He said he summoned every last bit of energy and flung his arm, miraculously connecting with the alarm.

My sister, Barb, and I received the call from the Emergency Room. Jack and I met her there. We waited all morning for some good news. It seemed that Daddy had a tear in his intestines and lost about eighty percent of his blood. They gave him transfusions, but he coded three times. The doctors were amazed that he survived. He was moved to the ICU[6] where we were finally allowed to see him. The doctors were not sure of his mental capacity. He was mumbling when we entered his room. I thought perhaps he had a near-death experience and saw Jesus or my mother. I waited expectantly to comprehend what he was saying. He would mumble and my sister would try to understand—are you in pain?—are you thirsty?—do you need something? "Yes! Call Leh's."

---

[6] Intensive Care Unit

Call Leh's??? Yes! Daddy wanted to be sure they knew he couldn't work that night. I guess I know where our family's work ethnic comes from.

Daddy faced months of recuperation. After a long hospital stay, we brought him home to our house, where we converted our living room into his bedroom. My sister and I took turns nursing him using all our vacation days. When that time ran out, Jack saved the day. Jack's doctor had recommended that he get a hemorrhoid operation and he had been procrastinating. Now was the time! He had surgery on a Friday and was well enough to watch Daddy by Monday. I still remember propping them both up against each other on the sofa and stressing—"Don't move. I'll be back at lunch time."

Fortunately, everyone recovered. My father always said that the doctors gave him the blood of a twenty-year old as he came back stronger than ever in body and in spirit! Again, many prayers were answered.

Life Lesson

My father received a second chance. His blood transfusions gave him new life. The shed blood of our Savior, Jesus Christ, gives us new <u>eternal</u> life!

> *. . . and have put on the new man*
> *who is renewed in knowledge*
> *according to the image of Him who created him,*
> Colossians 3:10

THE MARINES TO
THE RESCUE

In January of 1996, Daddy became ill and was hospitalized. My sister was scheduled for knee replacement surgery the next day. She and her husband lived just a short ride from the hospital. I volunteered to stay overnight with Daddy. Jack would sleep over at Barb's and drive her in for her morning surgery and pick me up.

It was a very long night. There was no sleeping in the uncomfortable chair and more stressful, no calming of Daddy's anxiety. He kept trying to get out of the bed. Prayer was the only course of action.

As the sun arose and I looked out the window, I could not believe my eyes. An historic event had occurred. Allentown, Pa. received a record snow fall. At least twenty-six inches of snow blanketed the area and enveloped everything. *All* the roads were closed. All the medical staff at the hospital were required to stay. No doctors or nurses were able to travel to the hospital to relieve them.

I was in shock and exhausted after a sleepless and stressful night. By mid-day, I called my sister and shared my predicament. A while later, she called me back and said that the Marines had been called in to assist with needed transportation. Assured that the nurses were taking good care of my father, I went down to the Administration Office and asked if I could be dropped off on one of their trips. The Marines were using Humvees. (These four-wheel-drive, all-terrain vehicles were only used by the military at that point in time.)

Next thing I know, I am walking down the hospital hallway heading to the exit flanked by Marines on either side. I felt like Dorothy in the *Wizard of Oz* going down the yellow brick road. I had always admired the Marines, but now they were my personal heroes.

It was a pretty exciting ride on snow-filled, empty roads. I was the last drop off. I asked the Marines if there was anything we could do to repay them. Anything that they needed? Any food? Anything? There was one thing—socks. They had been out in the snow all day and their socks were soaked. We called my sister with the request and as we pulled up close to her driveway, there stood Joe, my six-foot, four-inch brother-in-law, with his arms extended and his hands holding a dozen pairs of clean, dry socks.

To this day, Joe jokes that they traded me for a dozen pairs of socks!

Life Lesson

It is easy to overlook how God cares about every detail of our lives. He uses every situation to show his love and faithfulness. This time He used the Marines!

When roads seem to be closed, He will find a way for us.

> *I will sing of the mercies of the Lord forever;*
> *With my mouth will I make known Your faithfulness*
> *to all generations.*
> Psalm 89:1

THE LOSS OF A ROLE

This book is about life, faith, and family. I have shared a lot about my father's life and our family. You might wonder about Daddy's faith. Someone recently asked me if my father was "religious." If by religious you mean God-fearing and a believer, then yes. However, for most of his life he was not a regular church attender.

As I shared earlier, my mother was Catholic and my father Protestant. In order to marry, my father had to vow to bring up their children in the Catholic faith, which he did.

He rarely attended Mass with us and the occasions when he did were memorable. My First Holy Communion comes to mind. In those days, one needed to fast from midnight the night before Mass. I was at the end of the communion line, feeling very hot and weak, and totally lost consciousness. I awoke in the church vestibule listening to my father correcting the Mother Superior. He told her, "This is your fault. If only she would have been allowed to have some oatmeal, this would not have happened." (We never ever had oatmeal for breakfast, but I guess this is what Daddy thought would impress her.)

Through the years, my mother so wanted my father to convert to Catholicism. She prayed and prayed. About thirty years into their marriage, Daddy finally decided to go to the church rectory and declare his intention to convert. Unfortunately, he was told that since it was the Easter season, they were quite busy. He should come back at another time. That closed that chapter much to my mother's disappointment.

I know that faith played a huge role in my father's recovery from alcoholism and helped him through the grief of my mother's death. He would share with me how he prayed each night. In his later years, he did join a Protestant church and attended regularly. My father lived his faith by always being there—for his family and others. He was the "give you the shirt off his back" kind of person.

When my father was hospitalized in early January, 1996, he was never to return home. He needed gall bladder surgery but was too weak to withstand it. His organs failed one after the other making him weaker and weaker.

He reached the point when he could no longer speak. I remember being alone with him and telling him how much I loved him. He was conscious and stared into my eyes as I held his hand. Then he gave me his last sign of love as he slowly raised my hand to his lips and just kept kissing it.

Daddy passed away a few days later just a half hour after Jack and I had visited him. Perhaps it was too hard to leave this earth while we were there.

Again, I experienced the waves of grief wash over me again and again. In reflecting on the loss of my father, I realized that I was also grieving the loss of a role—the role of a daughter. It was one of my roles which I felt I had almost perfected.

Jack loved my father. At Daddy's funeral, he stood up and declared that Chet was the father he never had. (Although he had a wonderful mother, he was not so fortunate with his father.)

I will always thank God for the blessing of the parents He gave me. They are so much of who I am. I grieve their passing to this day. But I also find hope in the faith and heavenly inheritance which they left me and the expectation that I will see them again.

Life Lesson

I believe the greatest faith lesson my father taught me was his expression of the love of a father. Living life as the daughter of Chester Reinhard, my earthly father, taught me the reality of the love of my Heavenly Father.

> *Blessed be the God and Father of our Lord Jesus Christ,*
> *who according to His abundant mercy*
> *has begotten us again to a living hope*
> *through the resurrection of Jesus Christ from the dead,*
> 1 Peter 1:3

FINDING FAITH

As I write this book, *"Talks Under the Tiki Hut—the Sharing of Life, Faith, and Family,"* I imagine you and me sitting under the Tiki Hut telling each other memorable and pivotal life stories. As I reflect back over my life, I see how God was at work in every story—even the humorous ones! My intention is to specifically share those events that were crucial in building and evolving my faith. It has been my faith that has held me up during all the trials in my life.

I shared that after my mother's death, I decided that I believed! But how did that belief express itself? I continued to participate in the traditional church of my mother. Jack and I also raised the children in the faith. The focus was on Sunday church attendance, trying to follow the commandments—and confessing to a priest when we didn't.

Then I experienced a faith defining moment.

Our son, Joshua, was living in North Carolina in a Christian discipleship home for young men. I traveled there to visit. It had been a while since I had seen him. I so missed him and was very excited to see how he was doing.

We met in the living room of the home, and we sat facing each other—knees to knees. He leaned over and took my hands into his and shared, "Mom, I found Jesus." *(I'm thinking, of course you did, I've been taking you to church your whole life.)*

He was very enthused and passionately continued to tell me how Jesus was in his heart in a way he never knew before. *(I thought, that's wonderful for YOU honey! YOU need that. You have experienced so much difficulty in your nineteen years.)*

We attended Sunday service a couple of days later. Wow! I had never experienced people really worshiping God—so natural, spirit-filled and followed by a sermon straight from the Bible scriptures. I had the opportunity to meet a few of Josh's friends after service. Here was the common thread—they all had such JOY—regardless of their circumstances! And they talked about Jesus without whispering and as if they knew Him!

Life Lesson

Maybe Josh wasn't the only one who needed this Jesus. I really didn't understand how this faith differed so much from my traditional faith upbringing but this one thing I knew—I WANTED WHATEVER HE HAD!

> *Ask, and it will be given to you;*
> *seek and you will find;*
> *knock, and it will be opened to you.*
> Matthew 7:7

WHY ARE YOU SO FEARFUL?

I recently read a book about praying for our adult children. The author shared about her child who was using drugs. They sent him to rehab and miraculously, he was cured and "They lived happily ever after" *(my quote)*.

The story seemed so trite. This was <u>not</u> my experience nor that of several of my praying friends. Our son, Josh, had been battling drug addiction for twenty-five plus years. It had been a roller-coaster ride with many "highs" of sobriety and reconciliation, and many "lows" of addiction and estrangement. This ride has taken him through much pain and drama (detox, drug rehab, jail, accidents, and broken relationships)—Repeat . . . Repeat . . . Repeat. As his mother, I have taken that ride with him.

I can tell you that during all these years, I have come to know Jesus in a very real way and my faith has sustained me. I can't imagine going through life without faith. Jesus himself told us, "In this world you will have trouble."[7]

I am not alone in my experience with my son, several friends and acquaintances have also dealt with not just drug addiction but loss.

---

[7] John 16:33

One friend's twenty-something grandson was struggling with heroin use. His company paid for him to go to an expensive rehab. His family welcomed him back into their home. Weeks later, he was found in his car overdosed and deceased. The family left heartbroken and in shock.

Another friend lost her son to alcohol addiction. He was found in his condominium in Virginia. He had been hospitalized close to his family's home in Pennsylvania just a few months prior to his death. His parents and family begged him to go to rehab, but he felt he had his drinking under control and didn't need help. His mother was left to not only plan a funeral but to face and sort out all his financial and legal troubles. She shared that it was heart-wrenching to go through all his personal possessions. In addition, she had to prepare the condominium for sale. It was overwhelming. It delayed her grieving process and added stress on top of heartache. She has found comfort through her faith and also by attending support group meetings for the families of alcoholics.

One of my closest friend's daughter Tracy, had a drug problem. Eventually, Tracy moved to Boston and isolated herself from her family. My friend, Lynn, continued to encourage a relationship between her daughter and the rest of the family. Once a year, she would bring them together for a vacation. For them, it was not a vacation from the reality of the ongoing hurt, worry and heartache. Tracy would return to Boston and continue her drug use.

Then the dreaded day came when Lynn received the call that Tracy had overdosed and died. I drove Lynn to Boston to make the arrangements. First, we needed to clean out Tracy's apartment. We arrived there shortly after the Hazmat Team had removed Tracy's body which had gone unnoticed for days.

Again, another mother had the heart-wrenching experience of going through all her child's belongings and wondering what her last thoughts and words were. Wondering if this overdose was intentional or accidental. We cleaned out the apartment with Lynn taking numerous keepsakes.

The next morning, we arrived at the funeral home to pick up Tracy's ashes and take them back home for burial. Lynn had asked me to say a few prayers and have a little service. We really weren't expecting anyone to show up but to our surprise about a dozen people arrived.

I asked each of them to say a few words about their relationship with Tracy. It was truly a bitter-sweet service. Lynn had never met any of Tracy's friends but was comforted to know that there were people who loved her daughter and would mourn her passing as well. We all stood in a circle, held hands, and prayed for each other.

It's astonishing to me that I have this many personal, real-life examples to share with you. There are so many emotions that were felt by all these families. Of course, shock and denial. But also guilt and anger. Why? Why such a waste of a beautiful, young life? What else could I have done? What if? How could you do this to your family? How could you hurt us so? Don't you know how much we love you and how painful it is to lose you?

One of my greatest fears, is to receive "the call." It is the prayer of every parent who has a son or daughter in addiction not to receive "the call." My faith sustains me as well as the support and prayers I receive from my husband and friends.

Life Lesson

There is no recovery from addiction unless the addicted person wants to change.

> *But He said to them, "Why are you fearful,*
> *O you of little faith?"*
> *Then He arose and rebuked the winds and the sea,*
> *and there was a great calm.*
> Matthew 8:26

After Note

I have faith that the same Jesus, who was able to calm the winds and the sea can calm the storm and fear in my heart. For that, I am so thankful.

WHY READ THE BIBLE?

After our son, Joshua, went to the Christian discipleship program in North Carolina, he attended Mount Zion School of Ministry in Pennsylvania. It was so encouraging to see him healthy and doing so well. Once a month, visitors were welcomed to attend church service and a lunch fellowship. I visited as often as I could. Service was so sweet and genuine.

During this time, Josh was totally immersed in Bible study. He was learning so much and was super passionate about "The Word." When we were alone, he would encourage me to read the Bible. He was learning many things that we had not been taught, as well as teachings that contradicted our traditional faith. I felt so much spiritual tension and anxiety as Josh would argue these points. Could I really go against everything I was taught? The religion of my mother?

Josh was very convincing, but I still had many doubts. He gave me his study Bible[8] which had his name imprinted on the cover. I began to investigate for myself—an exploration that will no doubt continue until I breathe my last breath.

---

[8] *THE FULL LIFE STUDY BIBLE-KING JAMES VERSION* (Life Publishers International, 1992, 920-923)

Where to start? I quickly learned that the Bible is not like other books that you read from cover to cover sequentially. It contains history, poetry, chronicles of Jesus' life, letters, revelations and more.

The study Bible had footnotes that explained biblical-time terms or culture and cross referenced the Old and New Testaments. I found It impossible to read the New or Old Testament without referencing the other.

I had always thought that the Old Testament books were fables and stories for children like Noah and the Ark. Then I read in the book of Matthew[9] that Jesus talked of Noah! To believe in the Bible is to believe in its entirely. I came to comprehend that the Bible was inspired by God.

I also learned to pray to the Holy Spirit to guide me through God's Word to enlighten, convict and encourage me in my faith journey.

Did you ever question when someone says they have a "personal relationship with Jesus?" How can you have a relationship with someone you cannot see? The answer is simple—just like you develop a relationship with another person. Jesus speaks to you through His Word. You read, listen, reflect, and pray about how you might apply the Word to your life. This is how you get to know God. This is how you become a Christian—not just in a moment of salvation but in a lifetime and lifestyle.

Although there are sixty-six books by ~thirty authors spanning ~three-thousand years, there are no contradictions among them only validation. What is predicted in the Old Testament is revealed in the New Testament. In addition, archeological explorations have confirmed many Biblical facts.

I asked Pastor Jim how the Bible has affected his spiritual life. Below is his reflection (condensed and paraphrased):

> I feel that reading the Word of God enlightens me. I feel that it is always relevant. In Psalm 119, the writer says, 'Your Word I have hid in my heart. That I might not sin against You.' In my heart, not just in my mind.

---

[9] Matthew 24:37-38

Not just an intellectual understanding of the Word, but more of a spiritual connection.

For those who are new to reading the Bible, it can seem very complicated. For that reason, most Bibles are divided into chapters with numbered verses. In the back of the Bible, there is usually a dictionary or concordance which lists different topics. So if you are suffering from stress, anxiety, fear, or you're lonely, or you've got an addiction, or your hurting emotionally, you can look up that topic and it will list all the appropriate scriptures and their locations. At the beginning of my reading, I found this very helpful—to understand not just what I was thinking but what the Word of God said.

The Bible illuminates me by showing me the grandeur of life. So when I read, I not only see God but when I hear scriptures like the mountains trembled, and they shake and quake, and the oceans rise and fall, it shows me how God is not just a God of me, but of everything—even a little bird, God knows where it nests. God is so big and through the Word, I can see Him in life, in mountains, in storms, in sunny days and even in times of hurting and pain—I see Him to be the Comforter.

As you are reading this, I pray that you are excited by God's Word. If you have a Bible, I encourage you to read it. If you don't have one, please consider purchasing one. I read mine each morning. I gain strength and wisdom to face my day and peace and comfort to face life's troubles. Just as Adam and Eve walked with God in the garden and had sweet fellowship with Him, so too can we.

Life Lesson

I learned the most impressive concept to understand is that the Bible has one awe-inspiring, magnificent theme woven across and through all its books—God's great love for us and His goal to redeem us and spend all of eternity with us.

> *And truly Jesus did many other signs*
> *in the presence of His disciples,*
> *which are not written in this book;*
> *but these are written that you may believe*
> *that Jesus is the Christ, the Son of God,*
> *and that believing you may have life in His name.*
> John 20:30-31

CAN YOU BE BORN AGAIN?

M y intention with this chapter is not to be theological or give you a sermon but to share a pivotal turning point in my life. Without this chapter, much of the remaining chapters would not have come into being.

I had heard the term "Born Again" back in the 1970s, but I didn't really understand what it meant. I remember people coming to visit that had just been "Born Again." They were radical, aggressive and overbearing. I hid in the kitchen until they left. No more of that!

But after my newfound faith and Bible reading, I now yearned to understand. It may sound a little corny, but I purchased a book by the Rev. Billy Graham called—*"How to be Born Again*[10]*."* It was amazing. There are a few things that are still vivid in my memory although it has been many years since I've read it.

Rev. Graham shared how we all have an inward desire for God. That there is an emptiness within us that can only be filled by Him. As you may know, Rev. Graham traveled the world holding crusades where he shared the gospel and won many souls for Jesus. At one crusade in

---

[10] Billy Graham, *HOW TO BE BORN AGAIN* (Dallas: Word Publishing, 1977)

India[11], he learned that some people walked for as many as ten days, bringing their entire families—not because they had ever heard of Rev. Graham—some had never even heard of Jesus—but they had heard that a religious meeting was to be held. They had such a hunger to learn about God that they walked all those miles. Many stayed to find Christ.

As I read Rev. Graham's book, I longed to have that intimate relationship with God—that relationship that Adam and Eve had in the garden before they sinned, when they would walk with God in the cool of the day.

At the very end of the book, Rev. Graham answers the question—*"How are we born again?"*—when he extends an invitation to pray for forgiveness and ask Jesus to be our Lord and Savior.

I was at home sick from work the day I finished reading the book. I was alone in our bedroom when I felt led to get on my knees and pray that prayer with all sincerity and surrender. I waited, expecting something momentous and miraculous to happen—but no thunder or lightening, just a quiet peace.

I asked Pastor Jim what his experience was when he became born again. Below is his explanation (condensed and paraphrased):

> I didn't get the concept in the beginning either. My pastor explained the story of Nicodemus—a story that Jesus allowed to be placed in the Bible because it is one of the most beautiful stories[12]. Nicodemus, a Jewish ruler, came to Jesus by night and asked, "How can an old man be born again of his mother?" Jesus replies that you must be born again of the Spirit. You were born of water—of a woman—blood, water, but I need you to be born again of the spirit—the Spirit of God.
>
> It makes sense once we realize that each of us are really triune beings, made of body, soul and spirit. With our

---

[11] Graham, *HOW TO BE BORN AGAIN, 56-57*
[12] John 3: 1-31

body, we interact with the world—we see, hear, touch, taste, and smell. Our souls make us unique (give us the ability to think, feel and act). And thirdly, the spirit— our connection to God. I realized the importance of being born again by knowing that something was broken—that spirit, that friendship, that intimacy was broken.

How? When? It was the intimacy that Adam and Eve had before they sinned as they walked in the cool of the day with God. Eve told the serpent that God said that they should not eat of the fruit of the tree, or they would die. She ate of it, but did she die? No. What died was the sweet relationship they had with God. That's what was broken—the relationship. When we pray for repentance and accept that Jesus came to earth to pay the price for our sins, then that connection, that intimacy is restored, and we are born again! So many people know of God, but there needs to be a relationship a true communion of spirit—of love of God, passion for God.

I've been taught that salvation is a moment in time and a process. A moment that happens once you accept Jesus as your Lord and Savior—once you are born again, reconnected to God and a process that continues your whole life.

It is hard to explain. It was as if I could see things through God's eyes—what pleases Him—what grieves Him. The Holy Spirit convicts and encourages us and draws us closer to Jesus every day.

Up to that point, I must admit that I loved my wine! Some people can have a glass or two of wine with no problem. Not me! I found that there really wasn't enough wine to take away the deep pain and hurt that I had hidden in my heart from my past. And the more I would drink, the more depressed I would become. But *here* is the miracle—I totally lost the desire to drink. It was simply because I had so much peace in my soul that I didn't want to affect that in any way.

The Holy Spirit showed me other areas of my life that I needed to change. I had much to learn about how to be a disciple of Jesus.

Life Lesson

There was and is such joy to learn who Jesus really is and that He can be and is alive and relationally present in my life. This was a powerful pivotal turning point in my life. It has been an exciting adventure since then. I could never have predicted the challenges, opportunities, trials, and triumphs that were to come.

God has a purpose for each of us and I was about to learn mine.

> *And we know that all things work together*
> *For good to those who love God,*
> *To those who are the called according to His purpose.*
> Romans 8:28

IN SEARCH OF . . . PURPOSE

After my new faith experiences, I longed to find a church where I could hear Bible-based messages that would challenge me to change, grow spiritually and live my faith. I realized that I had attended the same church denomination for the first fifty years of my life. I wanted to broaden my horizon. I visited various churches for six months and was so encouraged when I found City Limits Assembly of God in Allentown, Pa. The preaching was dynamic, the people were so friendly—you couldn't get past the front door without a warm welcome and a hug. The church was also very diverse in culture and socio-economic standing. (One New Year's Eve service, a doctor's wife attended in her fur coat and also a homeless man.)

You might ask if you really need to participate in a formal church. Certainly, you can be a believer, read your Bible, and live a Christian life without a church. But the faith experience is so much richer in a church community environment. There is a fellowship and a faith family of support. How good it is to come together with like-minded believers to celebrate our faith! *Celebrate* not *attend*. Perhaps that's why the apostle Paul and others took their faith far and wide and opened many churches. That need still exists today. God made us to be relational—with Him and with others.

Pastor Jim Rivera and his wife, Deborah had been called into ministry in 1993. They arrived in Allentown, along with their two young children. Pastor Jim asked where they could find the poorest section of the city—that's where they wanted to serve. They found a beautiful old church in the middle of an impoverished neighborhood that was literally "on the other side of the tracks." Coincidentally, it was not far from the third-floor apartment where I grew up. Also, my grandfather who passed before I was born, owned and operated Joe Weber's Bar just two blocks from the church.

There were so many people in want—physically, emotionally, and spiritually. So much need—so many opportunities to serve. Over the years, Pastor Jim had many offers to move away to larger, more financially stable churches, but he insists that he was called once—to City Limits.

Deborah grew up in the church and as a little girl, watched and admired the Pastor's wife as she played the piano. Deborah always dreamed of being a Pastor's wife and her dream came true. (She also plays the piano!)

Pastor Jim has an amazing testimony. He was raised in North Philly, was involved in drugs, gangs, was stabbed, shot, and found on a park bench by David Wilkerson[13] who took him to Teen Challenge. There he found faith in Jesus, healing and sobriety. (Years later, Pastor Jim purchased that park bench from the city of Philadelphia, and it sits up front in the church—a constant reminder of God's love and mercy.) For years, the church operated a Timothy House for men inspired by Pastor Jim's love for men suffering with life issues.

Pastor Jim's story and his willingness to openly share it, created a culture at City Limits that was unusual—very real and encouraging—no facades. Many times, services ended with an invitation to share how God was working in our lives. Pastor Jim was and still is an encouragement to us and so many others. Little did I know when I found City Limits that

---

[13] An American Christian evangelist, best known for his book *The Cross and the Switchblade*. Also the founder of the addiction recovery program Teen Challenge and founding pastor of the non-denominational Times Square Church in New York City.

I not only found a church, but a mentor and forever friends in Pastor Jim and Deborah.

When I first joined City Limits, I was still working in corporate America. I started to serve in the church where I could—taught membership classes, served on the Church Board, was a Deaconess, and Women's Prison Ministry leader. Most of all, I just loved sharing my faith and encouraging others.

The Women's Prison Ministry was a real eye opener for me. We would visit once a month and provide a faith encouraging message to about twenty women who volunteered to attend. I had never understood how young women wind up in prison. What had their family life been like? One night, a young woman shared that "the drug dealers were my family!" How tragic. This experience taught me never to judge as we all didn't have the same parents.

It is so rewarding that years later, women come to City Limits, see me and give me an enthusiastic hug as they share, "Pastor Bev, I'm doing so well, and I have my children back." Honestly, I don't remember the names of most of them, but God does. He took the little seeds of faith that were planted and had them blossom. There is reason to celebrate!

More and more, I longed to retire and serve full-time in the ministry. In 2005, I was given the opportunity to retire early. What a blessing! I proclaimed that I was not *retired* but *refired*!

I longed to learn more and more about Jesus—who He really was and is. I started taking classes through Berean/Global University. Meanwhile, I used my corporate training and facilitating skills and assisted at church where needed. Our Associate Pastor moved on to lead his own church. Before I realized it, I was performing the Associate role. I was formally offered the position and I was so honored to serve. After twenty-five plus courses, and an internship, I became an ordained minister in 2012—a role to which I had never aspired.

I helped Pastor in most areas of the church and especially our outreaches. We had three large community events a year. Each involved enlisting donations and volunteers. Many of our corporate friends gave their time and talents. At our peak, each year we gave away four hundred plus turkeys for Thanksgiving and one thousand trees at Christmas. We wanted to <u>show</u> our poor community God's love. My husband, Jack, was very involved as well especially in the bike ministry. Old bikes would be donated, refurbished and given to some of the children. There were so many happy smiles on the children's faces, and on Jack's as well.

Each summer, we held a week-long evangelism event. With our matching, colorful, t-shirts, we would designate a city street for each team. We carried no Bibles. As Saint Francis said, "Preach the Gospel at all times and, when necessary, use words."

Each night, we would walk through the neighborhoods offering cold water, food, prayer, and invitations for week-end festivals for families and youth. The week culminated with outdoor water baptisms—an amazing experience! One year, we had two hundred plus volunteers from a North Carolina church. Most were teenagers who had never experienced inner-city evangelism.

One night as I was walking with my team, I noticed four or five young men standing on a porch. I felt a bit intimidated and was going to keep walking. Then my eyes connected with a young man's eyes. I could not keep walking. I walked over as he separated himself from the others and we met on either side of the porch railing. Very nervously, I asked, "Is there something that I can pray for you?" I was shocked when he replied, "Yes, that they don't shoot me." I quietly prayed for him right there and indirectly for my safety as well! I learned never to judge someone's heart. We all need prayer.

Looking back, I can see how God had prepared me along the way. In my corporate global training role, I traveled all over the U.S. and globally to Brazil, Mexico, Germany, England, France, and South Korea—places I never dreamed of visiting. I was blessed to make friends in each country and learned to appreciate the people, their culture and of course, their food.

I thought that God provided me with a college education and a career so I could afford to send my children to college. All the while, He was preparing me for ministry at City Limits and to an area where I had roots. I find no greater joy than to share about my faith and passion for God with you and others.

Life Lesson

In sharing this story, I can see how God has been guiding me toward His purpose for me. He has given me a heart and love for all His children— regardless of their age, color, or socio-economic standing. From the poorest to the richest, we all are God's children. Heaven is going to look like this!

> *May He grant you according to your heart's desire,*
> *And fulfill all your purpose.*
> Psalm 20:4

PLEASE PRAY

It was a usual day in my corporate life, attending yet another meeting. I was sitting in a large conference room, when my boss decided to call a break—a little strange since we had only just begun working our way through the extensive agenda. Soon I was the only person left in the room.

Surprisingly, my husband, Jack, suddenly appeared and closed the door. He pulled me close to him as I exclaimed, "Jack, we're at work!"

That's when life changed. He shared that he had bad news. Our twenty-five-year-old son, Josh, was in a motorcycle accident. Our son-in-law had gotten the call and informed Jack, who called the local hospital and tried to get more information. They summoned the chaplain to the phone! This could not be good news. All he could share was that Josh was still alive. We should come immediately to the Emergency Room (ER).

As we drove there, I called my Pastor and every friend I could think of and asked, "*Please Pray.*"

There were several miracles that happened that day. First, as we walked down the hall to the ER, I had an amazing feeling of peace. As a Mom, I can get pretty emotional when it comes to my children.

Although I was filled with fear, I literally felt as if God was walking behind me and placing His arms under mine and holding me up.

As we approached the ER, I saw Pastor Jim, who had beat us there. Finally, we got to see Josh. He was awake but very agitated. He sustained a serious head wound. His scalp was peeled back from his forehead to the middle top of his head—yet there was *no* concussion. Another miracle! The medical team was amazed. Pastor Jim prayed with Josh. I was so thankful that Pastor was there.

Josh had been riding his motorcycle down a fairly steep hill. Approaching the intersection, the sun blocked his view of the traffic light, and he propelled head-first through the rear passenger window of a car and somehow landed on the street pavement.

Just the night before, he and I had met for coffee at a local diner. I shared my concern for his safety on the bike. He assured me and actually showed me his expensive helmet and his special leather jacket with steel plates in the arms. Unfortunately, Josh was not wearing any of this gear the day of the accident. Consequently, he also severely damaged his one arm, leaving fragments of bone in his long-sleeved shirt.

Through all this, I was able to stay clear-headed and decisive. I had a call in to our local orthopedic group. Josh had had extensive back surgery a few years prior. I knew they also had a surgeon who specialized in the arm. I placed a call to the group and now we just needed to wait. Someone recommended that I take a little break, visit the cafeteria, and have a cup of coffee.

As I am standing in line, the gentleman to my right asks, "What are you doing here?" I looked up into the eyes of Josh's orthopedic back surgeon! I explained the whole situation. He set his lunch tray down, left it there and said, "Let's go up to the ER, I want to see Josh." I felt as if I was walking with an angel. What an amazing, caring doctor. He contacted his office and learned that the arm surgeon would not be available for a couple of hours. The back surgeon first checked out Josh's back, into which he had surgically placed a long rod a few years before. There was no damage! Another miracle. Personally, I lost track of the number of miracles, but God does not have limits.

The back surgeon then humbled himself and took Josh into pre-op where he carefully cleaned the arm wound and prepared him for surgery. The next day Josh spent his birthday in the hospital recovering.

Life Lesson

We never know what a new day will bring, but what I do know is that we can rely on God—for wisdom, for strength and for answered prayers and especially for miracles. I am forever thankful.

> *The Lord is my rock and my fortress and my deliverer;*
> *My God, my strength, in whom I will trust;*
> *My shield and the horn of my salvation, my stronghold.*
> Psalm 18:2

After Note

Several years later, Josh was living in North Carolina. On a Friday afternoon, I received another call from an Emergency Room. Josh had been trimming the trees on the church property when the chain saw kicked back into his face leaving a diagonal wound across the top of his nose and across his face. Another miracle—if it had cut one quarter of an inch deeper, it would have hit his brain and he would have died. As it was, the injury was not serious and he would be able to return to work the following Monday. Meanwhile, Jack and I decided to drive down from Pennsylvania to make sure he was okay.

We went straight to the construction building where he worked. Several women from his church whom I knew worked in the office and greeted us. Josh was in the back of the building, and they summoned him. They were quite anxious and worried. All I heard was, "Miss Beverly, Mr. Jack, please prepare yourselves, Josh's injury looks quite bad. Now please Miss Beverly, brace yourself." I had a huge knot in my stomach as we waited for him to arrive. And then he appeared. Jack and I looked at Josh and then looked at each other, looked at Josh and looked at each other and said, "Not bad!" In comparison to his motorcycle accident, his injury was "Not bad!" How bad must it be if your son takes a chain saw to the face and it's, "Not bad!"?

Surely, God had his hand on my son.

HAPPY BIRTHDAY . . . I THINK

It was a milestone birthday for me. One which might call for a party or a special restaurant dinner but—there was a conflict. My husband Jack's Trout Unlimited[14] (TU) Chapter was also having a special day—an anniversary, complete with a fund-raising dinner. I didn't really mind going to the TU dinner. Many of our friends would attend and there was sure to be fun.

As part of the fundraiser, they conducted a raffle. If you have not participated in such a raffle, I'll explain how it works. Jack was in charge of soliciting items, donations of goods or services from local businesses that would be raffled off with the proceeds going to Trout Unlimited. He did a really good job and had about one hundred and fifty different prizes. Each item was placed on a series of tables along with a paper bag. Tickets were sold. Participants would then peruse the tables; decide which item or items they were interested in, and place one half of their ticket in the appropriate paper bag. At the end of the night, Jack would

---

[14] **Trout Unlimited** is an American non-profit organization dedicated to the conservation of freshwater streams, rivers, and associated upland habitats for trout, salmon, other aquatic species, and people.

visit each bag and draw the winning ticket. Anticipation rose as dinner was completed and raffle time arrived.

As it happened, two of our granddaughters, Jacquelyn and Isabelle, were there and Pop Pop Jack enlisted them to be his assistants and the official ticket drawers.

Unbeknownst to me, Jack had also perused all the prizes, identified an item that he thought would be to my liking, bought tickets, and placed all his tickets in the appropriate bag. So sweet, right?!

Item by item, table by table, Jack moved along, had a granddaughter pull a ticket and he would call the winning number. I must admit it took a *really* long time. Of course, I didn't have a clue that Jack was hoping to win something special for me. So, they came upon his selected item, Jacquelyn pulled the ticket and Jack with much excitement, announced that he had won! He brought the prize to me and with the microphone still in hand, exclaimed, "Happy Birthday, Honey!" The prize was a beautiful powder blue golf shirt.

After he was done raffling all the prizes, he came over and asked how I liked the golf shirt. I really liked it—so much so that it looked familiar to me. I shared that I thought I had one *just like it*! In fact, it was hanging in our laundry room at home. With that said, Jack's face turned from one of glee to gloom. Imagine this—he had hung all the clothing prizes in the laundry room until the night of the fundraiser. When he went to scoop up all the donated, hanging items, he also scooped up my recently laundered powder blue golf shirt! No wonder I liked it! I don't know when we had laughed so hard! What are the odds of Jack taking my shirt, placing all his tickets in one of one hundred and fifty bags, and out of so many tickets having a granddaughter pull his ticket? So basically, he won me my own shirt.

Our friends, who witnessed the whole spectacle, still talk and laugh about this story to this day! Since then, Jack has been sure to bless me with more original birthday gifts but none so funny as the powder blue golf shirt.

Life Lesson

Another humbling experience? Don't hang prizes in the Laundry Room?

Seriously, I do believe that God delights in all our experiences. He wants us to love Him and each other. What a sweet and memorable expression of love and thoughtfulness—the powder blue golf shirt.

> *A cheerful heart is good medicine…*
> Proverbs 15:13a

A MOTHER'S LOVE

There is such a bond created between a mother and her child. I remember when I saw Dennine for the first time. I had waited six years to conceive my "heart's desire" and indeed my heart was overwhelmed with love for her. She was so pretty even as a newborn and I was so thankful to be a mother—the only role I truly desired.

When Josh was born four years later, he was square—yes, as wide as he was long—nine chunky pounds of cuteness. Seconds after birth, he clasped my index finger and wouldn't let go. My heart melted.

When Jack and I married, I also married his two children, J. D. and Monica. I often joke that they are my favorites—they gave me no stretch marks! I never really accepted the term "stepchild." Since Jack and I raised them, I always considered them mine although I did occasionally have to share them with their biological mother. I have come to appreciate how important it was and is for them to have a relationship with her.

When the grandchildren arrived, there were definitely no "steps" involved. There are no step-grandchildren! When people ask us whose child or grandchild it is, Jack and I respond "ours." We choose to love them all the same. We have eight grandchildren, Zachery, Julia, Michael, Sara, Jacquelyn, Isabelle, Genevieve, and Sebastian and we love them all! Each is so unique with special gifts given from God. We have been blessed with our first great-granddaughter, Kinsley. I'm a *great*-grandmother—not bragging, just the facts!

When Jack and I married, we had physical custody of all four of our children with weekend visitation with their other parents. Shortly after we married, Josh, who was then eight years old, decided to move in with his Dad—a decision that broke my heart. I remember sobbing in Jack's arms in our garage after Josh rode away.

Josh was a gifted athlete and was encouraged to focus on sports. As he grew older, sports were always the focus. He excelled in football, baseball, and wrestling. No need to focus on grades, working, or chores. There was little accountability or boundaries.

Josh's drug addiction started when he was a teenager. When Josh went to his first rehab, the whole family went to visit him and share our feelings. We hoped that this outpouring of support would influence his recovery. I remember Monica crying as she shared and how Josh's Dad observed that she summed up the feelings well for all of us.

Addiction definitely impacts the whole family. I read an article in our local newspaper that interviewed a mother who had recently lost a child to drugs. She explained that drug addiction is like shrapnel—it explodes in many directions with everyone being injured. There are so many families whose hearts are shattered by addiction. The opioid "crisis" has become a hot topic but unfortunately with little or no solutions or hope for families.

As a Christian, I have seen how faith in Jesus Christ has the power to transform, heal, and create that new man or woman of God. [15]

Many rehab programs now seek financial support from the government and prohibit the name of Jesus or the Holy Spirit—the exact sources of power that are needed.

As humans, we are comprised of body, soul, and spirit. Many programs focus on the physical addiction and ignore the spiritual. For total healing to take place, attention needs to be on the physical, the

---

[15] Ephesians 4:20-24

emotional roots of the addiction and most importantly, the spiritual hope that can only come from a loving, caring and powerful God.

One night many years ago, I was at a church service and during worship I felt emotionally overwhelmed. Pastor Jim encouraged us all to clear our minds and just worship God. As I did that for a few minutes, I heard a voice clearly say, "I love him too". I knew I heard God's voice. It was a statement that I would never have conjured up in my mind, "I love him too". It reminded me that although I am Josh's mother, God is his Heavenly Father. How humbling . . . how reassuring.

One of the by-products of drug addiction is co-dependency. According to Wikipedia, "Codependency is a behavioral condition in a relationship where one person enables another person's addiction, poor mental health, immaturity, irresponsibility, or under-achievement". How one enables can vary. As a mother, it is very difficult not to feel responsible for your child. After caring for them as babies and young children, teaching them, feeding and clothing them, it is difficult to know exactly when or how to turn that off. For years, I struggled with this. The best summary description of codependency I have found is when you do something for your child that they can and should do for themselves. Divorce also played into my codependency issues as I felt guilt and lack of control as a parent making it easier for me to make life easier for Josh.

During the years, Jack and I had numerous counseling sessions with Pastor Jim—not only our pastor but a dear friend. He had been "clean" for decades. During one session, Pastor Jim looked me in the eyes and said, "Bev, if I lived in your house, I would still be an addict." What a convicting punch to the heart! Josh wasn't the only one who needed to change. I did too!

Children need consequences. Without boundaries and rules they are left to their own devises which are usually undependable. It is one of the hardest challenges to sit back and watch your child going down the wrong path. However, when we enable them, it does not help. It only prolongs their recovery.

A few years ago, I taught a class for a small group of women on setting boundaries with our adult children. Honestly, it was for me as well as for them. It was healthy to share our stories, encourage each other, and learn to lean on God instead of ourselves.

One of the class exercises was to bring in two photos of our child—one as a little boy or girl and a current one. What we learned was that, as mothers, we tend to think of our children as the sweet, innocent little ones they were. But we need to file that image in our memories and face the reality of who they are now. This small group of women still has a strong bond, and we pray for each other's children.

A few years ago, Josh gave me a beautiful statue[16] (see below) with the inscription "A Mother's Love." Josh said, "You deserve it Mom." As I clasped my hand around it and held it to the air, I felt as if I just received an Oscar, but instead of thanking the Academy and my family, I thanked my God!

A Mother's Love Statue

---

[16] Made by the artist, Jim Shore.

I believe that Jesus had His hand on each of my children from the moment of conception. His love for them is even greater than a mother's love.

Life Lesson

Being a mother is a great challenge and responsibility. We must learn that love for our children is not enough. We need to ask God for wisdom to create healthy boundaries and teach responsibility. We must never forget that God loves them too! Be sure they know.

> *For You formed my inward parts;*
> *You covered me in my mother's womb.*
> Psalm 139:13

THOUGHTS FROM
A THREE-YEAR-OLD
GRANDDAUGHTER

We offer a week-long Vacation Bible School every year at my church. It was scheduled in the evening as many of our volunteer teachers worked during the day.

When my first granddaughter, Julia, was three years old, her parents allowed me to enroll her. We both looked forward to it. Each night, I would pick her up early so we could go out to eat at McDonald's and then head down to church.

One night as we were driving (and had <u>not</u> been talking about God at all) I hear this little voice coming from the car seat in the back of the car.

"Nana, what are you going to do in heaven without me?" I was taken back and asked, "Julia, what do you mean?" She replied, "Well Nana, it's going to take a *really, really, really* long time for me to get old!"

Tears started to fill my eyes as I thought that this sweet little child was imagining a time when we would not be together.

I told her that I would just have to wait for her.

Afterthoughts

I believe that children have a keen spiritual sense, an awareness that unfortunately seems to dissipate over time.

Fast Forward

*Recently, I was speaking with Julia, who is now nineteen years old and a mother. I reminded her of our conversation when she asked me, "What are you going to do in heaven without **me**?"*

*She said if I were in heaven, she would now ask, "Nana, what am I going to do on earth without **you**."*

> *Tears are again filling up my eyes!*
> *I'm so thankful for our relationship and thank God for her.*

Life Lesson

Never underestimate the spiritual awareness of a child. Also, although we are mortal, we have hope and salvation in Jesus Christ. With faith and belief, we will see our loved ones again.

> *And God will wipe away every tear from their eyes; there shall be no more death, nor sorrow, nor crying. There shall be no more pain, for the former things have passed away."*
> Revelations 21:4

A TEST OF FAITH

"I have a lump." The words you never want to hear from your grown daughter. It was Thanksgiving Day and we had just finished the holiday feast at our house. Our oldest daughter, Dennine, asked if she could speak with us alone. We wondered the reason as we walked into our bedroom and closed the door. There she shocked us with the news that she had found an olive-sized lump in her breast. She tried to calm us by sharing that she was going for a biopsy right after the holiday—it was probably nothing serious given her age of thirty-five. We prayed so hard for a good diagnosis.

In a few days, the call came—"Mom, I have cancer." I literally dropped to my knees in disbelief. How could this be? She was so young, thirty-five years old—too young to even have had her first mammogram. And she had young children—Julia-eight, Michael-six, and little Sara only two. No one in our family had ever had breast cancer. I prayed, "Oh God, please let it be me—give me the cancer—not my daughter." I had experienced many trials and losses in my life, but this was one I could never have anticipated.

Dennine was my first, long-awaited child. So loved. I had tried very hard to protect her from all harm even before she was born. In the early seventies, as it is now, the tradition was to give the mother-to-be a baby shower. Many times the gifts were not only decorated with wrapping paper and bows, but also baby rattles. As I prepared for her upcoming birth, I carefully washed all her clothing gifts. I also put all the baby rattles, submerged them in a large pot of boiling water and sterilized them—nothing was going to harm my baby! The good news—the germs were definitely killed. The bad news—all the rattles, made of plastic, melted into one large clump, one which would never rattle again! I had so wanted to be the "perfect" mother—an unattainable aspiration for sure.

As an adult, Dennine appeared to be so healthy. She ate a healthy diet, exercised regularly and even taught a bicycle spinning class. She had earned her Bachelor's and Master's of Education and really enjoyed teaching elementary school. Her students loved her. She had so much to contribute.

Dennine's cancer was a very aggressive type, and she was scheduled for a lumpectomy as soon as possible. It was a blessing that she had found the lump early and sought treatment. Fortunately, the cancer had not spread to her lymph nodes. With a regiment of chemotherapy and radiation treatments her prognosis was very good.

She was very brave insisting to go to the chemo treatments alone. (A decision with which I was not happy.) She never stopped teaching. She would go for treatments on a Thursday and be really sick over the weekend. Jack and I would pick up the children on Fridays after school and return them Sunday night, so they were really spared from seeing their Mom so sick.

Dennine had the most beautiful perfect hair—long, brown and wavy—not too curly or too straight. Since she began to lose her hair, she asked her husband, Paul, to shave it all off for her. Unbeknownst to her, Julia, her eight-year-old daughter, found the remnants in the wastebasket, and saved a lock. So sweet!

Dennine, her most-supportive husband, and I went wig shopping. They had the most adorable wigs and she looked absolutely beautiful in the one she purchased. Although I kept reassuring her, she said I was her Mom and of course, I thought the wig looked great. The next day, she accompanied Paul on a business trip to New Jersey. She had to call me to share that three different women (strangers) had stopped her and complimented her on her haircut. One even asked to take a photo. Conclusion—Moms are usually right!

During this time, I must be honest. I had great fear, worry and yes, even some doubt. But I treasure this trial in the sense that it grew my faith. I knew that whatever the outcome, God would see me through.

Dennine's treatments were successful! She regularly goes for checkups. She has also become an inspiration for many other women. In our area, they conduct a yearly run for breast cancer awareness and fundraising. The first year she participated with a small team. Recently, the group has grown to at least fifty women. We celebrate that she is one of the ten plus year survivors! Thank you, God.

Life Lesson

I have learned that we become closest to God when we face a situation or trial over which we have no control. In our society, we are taught to be so independent. In our culture, we are encouraged to pull ourselves up by the bootstraps! When none of these options work and we realize that we truly have no control over the circumstances, that is when we learn what real faith is—how to depend upon God and not ourselves!

> *For God has not given us a spirit of fear,*
> *but of power and of love and of a sound mind.*
> 2 Timothy 1:7

PLANTING SEEDS OF FAITH

I *love* my children—but my grandchildren—I'm *in love* with them. The words are indescribable—to see your children's children. By the way, there are no "step" grandchildren. We were blessed with eight beautiful grandchildren, each unique, special, talented, and precious in their own way. And all loved so much.

There is so much to teach them. They're like little sponges. Of course, they are always observing not just what we say, but what we do. Our most important job is to sow the seeds of faith into these fertile little souls.

I purchased a little Pre-School Bible, and I would read them stories especially at bedtime. Seeing the Bible through their eyes increased my faith as well. I remember Julia's reaction when we first read the story of how Jesus calmed the storm. He said, "Stop wind, stop waves and they did." Julia's beautiful, innocent, little blue eyes opened wide as she exclaimed *"WOW!"*

Life Lesson

As adults, we sometimes lose the wonder of who Jesus is and how powerful He was and is. Seeing the Bible through the eyes of a child will increase your faith as well as theirs.

> *Then Jesus called a little child to Him,*
> *set him in the midst of them,*
> *and said, "Assuredly, I say to you,*
> *unless you are converted and become as little children,*
> *you will by no means enter the kingdom of heaven.*
> *Therefore whoever humbles himself as this little child*
> *is the greatest in the kingdom of heaven.*
> Matthew 18:2-4

I'M NOT AN ARTIST!

Jack and I have been blessed to spend the winter months in Key Largo, Florida for the last ten years. One of the first years we were there, we attended a Sunday breakfast hosted by the Men's Club. A very sweet woman, Sally, sat next to me and we began to converse. She asked me what I planned to do while I was vacationing there. I explained that I brought along my charcoals and some watercolor paints from my college art class and I wanted to practice drawing and painting. Although the art class was decades ago, I recalled how relaxing art was. Somehow, it turned down the logical, left side of your brain and turned up the creative, right side. Please note—*no one* had ever expressed any encouragement or provided any compliments regarding my ability or class efforts. No matter—my goal now was just to relax.

My answer ignited much enthusiasm from Sally and she exclaimed, "You *must* come to the Purple Elves." At least that's what my one, good-hearing ear heard (scarlet fever as a child had left me deaf in one ear.)

Meanwhile, I'm pondering to myself, "What is a Purple Elf?" What she actually said was, "You must come to the Purple Isles." In reality, it was the "Art Guild of the Purple Isles," a group of artists from the Florida Keys who met regularly, attended art classes, encouraged each other's talents, conducted art shows, and promoted art throughout the Keys.

I could clearly see that Sally had misunderstood me. "I'm not an artist!" I explained. That didn't seem to deter Sally and she invited me to the next Guild meeting. She was so nice, I couldn't say no.

At the meeting, the Board reviewed all the upcoming events one of which being the Florida Keys Mosaic. Everyone was given a four-inch by four-inch canvas and instructed to paint something representative of the Keys. The painting needed to be turned in by a certain date at which time the hundred plus canvases would be combined into a vertical mosaic wall. The mosaic would then "tour" the major towns from Key Largo to Key West to promote art. What an awesome idea! Not for me, however. As they handed out a small canvas to each person, they insisted I take one. It needed to be handed in at the local art store. But "I'm not an artist."

Now I was far from relaxed. How did I get myself into this situation? I had the solution—I would just go to the art store and hand back the blank canvas. I explained, "I'm not an artist." One of the guild members whom I had just met overheard me, took me by the arm and, along with the art store owner, showed me some of the recent entries. One by one, they pulled canvases out of a large cardboard box and said that surely I could do better than this one or that one. Needless to say, I walked out of the art store with a blank canvas in hand. "I'm not an artist!" (Nobody was listening!)

Not only wasn't I relaxed, now I was stressed with a big knot forming in my stomach. So what were my choices? I decided to give it a try. I had been admiring a beautiful palm tree outside our house and decided it would be my subject. Forget the charcoal. The canvas must be painted. Usually watercolor paints were used with watercolor paper. So here I am with an acrylic-type canvas and my watercolor paint. Amazingly, I did it! The painting actually did look like a palm tree. I turned it in on time.

A few weeks later, a reception was held at the Civic Center where the finished mosaic was beautifully displayed including my little palm tree.

Palm Tree

My husband was so proud that he would seek out total strangers and bring them over to see his wife's creation. So sweet!

What an unintentional start as an artist. Don't misunderstand—I would still declare, "I'm not an artist" but the Guild has given me wonderful opportunities to meet people who really are artists and to take classes in various mediums. I do try!

For years, I would attend and volunteer at the annual Art Show but not enter any of my work. One year, a good friend so encouraged me that I did enter one piece. Drumroll—Here's where a great ending to the story would be that I won an award! Not so. We did have to write an "Artwork Inspiration Statement" to help attendees understand what the painting was trying to say. I have included the statement along with a photo of the painting on the last page of this chapter.

I was volunteering at the welcome desk when one of my friends asked the location of my show entry. After seeing it, she returned to me and without saying a word, kissed the top of my head. I guess, "I'm still not an artist."

Life Lesson

God gives us different talents. Painting taught me to stick to writing!

> *Therefore humble yourselves under the mighty hand of God, that He may exalt you in due time,*
> 1 Peter 5:6

Artwork Inspiration Statement
"Sweet Youthful Memories"

I have such wonderful memories, as a child, of being in the flower garden with my mother. She was such a sweet woman and her flowers seemed to adore her and grow beautifully under her care. She would faithfully tend to them, and they rewarded her with fabulous blossoms.

I distinctly recall the huge flower bed filled with beautiful blue hydrangeas that graced the side of our home. I would love to help my mother water them and just spend special time together with her.

I lost my mother when I was twenty-seven years old. Now, I grow beautiful blue hydrangeas that grace the side of our home. As I water and tend to them, I feel my mother's presence right there with me.

I am blessed to have five granddaughters—Julia, Sara, Jacquelyn, Isabelle and Genevieve. A few summers ago, I held a "Granddaughters' Day." We picked the beautiful blue hydrangeas, and I taught the girls how to make pretty floral arrangements which they gave to their mothers as gifts.

Hopefully, I have created some sweet, youthful memories for them to share in the years to come.

Painting of Hydrangeas

WHERE'S MILTON?

A few years ago, we were all saddened to hear of the passing of one of our congregation, and a member of our Worship Team. Milton was a faithful servant of our church although he was known for being late for everything.

Milton's family was from New York and would be traveling to Allentown for the 6:00 p.m. church service. Milton was cremated at a funeral home just a few blocks from the church.

As the Associate Pastor, I came in early to see if Pastor Jim needed any assistance. I found him, along with Milton's family, in Pastor's office right off the church sanctuary. They had been trying to reach the funeral home but to no avail. They were concerned as Milton's ashes had not been delivered to the church for the service. I assured them that I would work with the funeral home, and they could continue to discuss the format of the impending memorial service.

I walked through the sanctuary and into the church foyer. It was about 5:00 p.m. and fortunately, no one had yet arrived for the service. I called the funeral home and was connected to their after-hours voice mail. Yikes! Now I was getting nervous.

I left a message sharing the urgency of the matter. We needed Milton's ashes! Now. Please, please, please call me back.

People started filing in for the service—still no call from the funeral home. Finally, the phone rings. It was the funeral director. There obviously had been a miscommunication. They promised to transport Milton's ashes to the church as soon as they could send someone down to the city.

It was now 6:00 p.m. and Pastor Jim started the service. Thankfully, a man from the funeral home arrived and gently placed the urn into my hands and left. Now, there I was, in the church foyer all alone—except for Milton. Just me, holding Milton's urn.

What do I do? It wasn't like a wedding where I could walk Milton down the center aisle to the altar! I was able to contact one of the men from our church. I asked him to meet me in the foyer, take the urn outside, around the side door and into the back door of Pastor Jim's office. I entered the sanctuary and, as unobtrusively as possible, made my way to Pastor Jim. At an opportune time, I whispered in his ear, "Milton is in your office."

Pastor continued with the service and at just the perfect moment, as he was speaking about Milton, he stepped into his office and emerged ever so gracefully with the urn. It was a flawless, sweet transition and the service continued. Milton truly was a man who was late for his own funeral!

Life Lesson

There are just some things that they do not teach you in ministry school! That's when you really need to rely on the Holy Spirit.

> *Now may the God of hope fill you*
> *With all joy and peace in believing,*
> *That you may abound in hope*
> *By the power of the Holy Spirit.*
> Romans 15:13

MUST LOVE AUDIO TEXT

A couple of years ago, I received a call from Pastor Jim. He shared that he was in a lot of pain and had a bad case of gout (a disease that causes an inflammation in the bones and episodes of acute pain).

It was a Wednesday night when we usually have our mid-week service. He asked if I could please cover for him. Of course! As I wondered what sermon I might share, I thought I should call the others on the ministry staff and let them know Pastor's situation.

I was upstairs in my office and decided to send them a text message. I often use the audio/voice text to quickly dictate a message. You select a little microphone icon, speak your message, and it is automatically typed for you. Very cool!

I selected the microphone icon and said, "Good afternoon, ministers. I just wanted to let you know that Pastor Jim will not be at service tonight as he has a severe case of gout."

I was about to press the send arrow when fortunately, I read over the message. I must have laughed for several minutes until I could finally compose myself.

The message actually read, "Good afternoon ministers. I just wanted to let you know that Pastor Jim will not be at service tonight as he has a severe case of *doubt*."

That night in my message, I preached about faith and doubt and shared this little story as my introduction and the scripture at the bottom of this page as my sermon.

Life Lesson

As a pastor, if you have a serious case of doubt, by all means stay home! Fortunately, Pastor Jim only had gout.

> *But let him ask in faith,*
> *with no doubting,*
> *for he who doubts is like a wave of the sea*
> *driven and tossed by the wind.*
> James 1:6

A SWEET DOVE

I wonder if I would be in ministry today without the teaching, encouragement, and example of my Pastor and good friend, Pastor Jim Rivera. Pastor Jim truly has a heart to serve God and love His people.

Several years ago, a young, single woman became pregnant and sadly, lost the baby at the end of the pregnancy. She asked Pastor Jim to perform the funeral. Trying to make the service as uplifting as possible, he asked his secretary to stop at the pet store and purchase a small, white dove. Pastor did not want the young woman's last memory to be looking down into the ground.

Towards the end of the grave-side service, Pastor stooped down to open the little cage, and ever so gently removed the dove. He then cupped his two hands around the bird. Bending over, he extended his arms almost to the ground and with all the energy he could muster, quickly raised his arms skyward and released the bird into the heavens. Shockingly, the bird jettisoned to the earth just as quickly as he had been propelled into the sky. Plop!

Not to be deterred, Pastor Jim was determined to release the bird. Now all eyes were on the bird. He gently picked up the bird (who was thankfully still alive!) and repeated his actions—cupped his hands gently around the bird, bent over, extended his arms almost to the ground and mustering up rocket-like energy, thrust the bird skyward. Again, the dove plunged to the ground. Come to find out, the dove's wings had been clipped!

After Note

Pastor Jim did achieve his goal—no one was looking down at the ground, all eyes were on the dove. Most people watching tried hard to contain their amusement.

The Sweet Ending

The young woman who lost her baby adopted the little dove. She named him Angel, the same name she had given to her little baby. She took the little dove home as her companion and comfort—a reminder of how much God loves her. An ending sweeter than Pastor ever imagined.

Life Lesson

In Genesis 8 (see below), the dove, with its fresh olive leaf was used as a sign of life after the Flood so Noah knew it was safe for his family and his animals. The little dove in our story was used as a sign of life after the waters of grief subsided. God is our Comforter!

> *He also sent out from himself a dove, to see if the waters had receded from the face of the ground . . . Then the dove came to him in the evening, and behold, a freshly plucked olive leaf was in her mouth; and Noah knew that the waters had receded from the earth.*
> Genesis 8:8,11

SO PROUD

Background

Twenty months prior, Julia sent a text to her Nana asking if they could meet as soon as possible. Of course. Julia had recently returned from her freshman year at Penn State University. She wanted to attend school closer to home and family. Her grandmother was concerned with Julia's stress level with all the changes and wondered what could be so urgent . . .

Months later . . .a conversation between Nana and Julia, her oldest granddaughter:

Nana said:

> Julia, of all the things you will ever accomplish in your life—degrees, jobs, success—the thing that I will always be most proud of is your decision to keep your baby.

Julia replied:

> But Nana, I don't understand. Why would you be proud me? It was the right thing to do. If I choose to not kill my annoying, younger brother tonight, would you be proud of the fact that I didn't?

Nana explained:

> Julia, this was a moral decision you made. In this day and age, many young women would have chosen differently, selfishly. They might have said, 'I don't want to ruin my life—my college life, my career, my future'. They would have made what seemed like the easier choice. But you never wavered. There were people who didn't agree with your decision. Right?

Julia:

> Yes.

Nana:

> People who thought abortion was the easier solution.

Julia:

> Yes.

Nana:

> But you were not influenced. You made a huge moral decision. It reflects who you are—who you are as a person. You have a wonderful, sweet, caring heart! I love you for that and I am so proud of you.
>
> Because of that decision, God blessed you with the most precious little girl, Kinsley Paige—our first great granddaughter.

Life Lesson

This sweet little baby was born weighing just one pound, nine ounces. She spent two months in the Newborn Intensive Care Unit (NICU) with her dedicated parents by her side the whole time. She fought a brave fight for her life continuing as her mother had done for her. She is now a healthy, bright, fun little three-year old. God cares for life while inside or outside the womb. We are blessed!

For You formed my inward parts;
You covered me in my mother's womb.
I will praise You, for I am fearfully and wonderfully made;
Marvelous are Your works,
And that my soul knows very well.
Psalm 139:13-14

WHO'S BURIED IN GRANT'S TOMB?

J ack and I have been preparing our final funeral arrangements. Not that we think we are going home to Jesus anytime soon, but we want to relieve our children of such a planning burden.

As part of our preparation, we purchased burial plots right next to my parents. So placed from left to right are my father, then my mother then my plot, follow by Jack's.

Several months ago, Jack and I were visiting my parents' graves. I was standing at the far left and Jack at the far right. As I glanced across the four plots, I gasped! "Jack, look at our plots!" "What," he questioned?

"The grass on our plots is new, light green," I shared in horror and amazement. "I think they buried someone in our plots!"

Of course, it was a Saturday, and no one was available to call at the cemetery office. All weekend we wondered what their answer would be. First thing Monday morning, I called the office and with much angst, explained our concern that we feared people were buried in our plots by mistake. The woman replied, "Oh, no worries. We opened the plots and buried the cement vaults that will hold your caskets. That way if you pass during the winter, when the ground is frozen, we will be able to access the graves." Wow. Who knew! We were understandably relieved.

Life Lesson

As a Christian, I believe that "to be absent from the body, is to be present with the Lord." Of course, it is much more important to know where your spirit will go than your body. We should prepare our whole life for our spiritual, after-death destination.

In the book of Luke, he recounts how "the good thief" who hung next to Jesus on the cross, believes that Jesus is the Son of God. Jesus assures him of where he will be.

> *And Jesus said to him, "Assuredly, I say to you,*
> *today you will be with Me in Paradise."*
> Luke 23:43

I'LL CATCH HIM

I have procrastinated writing this chapter as it is one of the most painful, revealing stories. It is also one of the most powerful and faith proclaiming.

I shared with my son, Josh, that I was writing this book. I told him how I found it difficult to share about my faith journey without sharing not only about his faith but also about his drug addiction. I explained to him that I would like him to review any stories in which he is mentioned. He replied, "I don't need to review any of it. Write it all—all the darkness—then the light will shine all the brighter." Still, I struggle to write. If you and I were alone sitting under the Tiki Hut, I know I could easily share about God's mercy, love, and redemption but to take ink to paper somehow makes this story all the more real and in fact, should make it all the more encouraging. So, here goes . . .

Several years ago, for one of the anniversaries of "9/11," there were many TV shows remembering and commemorating the events of that tragic day. One of the stories that is forever seared into my mind and heart was the narrative of "The Falling Man." Unbelievably, numerous people jumped to their deaths from the Twin Towers in order to escape the intense heat and flames. Video audio captured the horrific sound as a body would hit the ground. The Associated Press captured one of these tragic souls, falling midair, arms and legs flailing about. Later, a search was made to identify the man. Although his sneakers and clothing were somewhat recognizable, no identification was ever made.

As I watched in horror, fear gripped my heart as I thought about my son, Josh, and drug addiction. I thought, "That photo is like my son. He is free falling and he is going to crash." Just then, I heard a voice say, "I'll catch him." There was no doubt that I clearly heard God's voice. "I'll catch him!" That is not a phrase that I would have even imagined or thought of on my own.

Addiction is such a strange and cruel disease. If your child had cancer or some other life-threatening sickness, you would love them, take care of them, physically and financially—any way you could. And they would probably be appreciative. But drug addicts, in order to support their addiction will use many hurtful means—lying, stealing, manipulating.

I remember one time Jack and I were out of town and Josh called and asked if he could borrow our two kayaks which were in our backyard. He was going kayaking with one of the men from our church. I thought this was great—getting out in nature and with someone who could be such a good influence. As a mother, I so *wanted* to believe good things for my son. A few days later, we learned that Josh had sold the kayaks.

I must admit that many times we gave or "loaned" him money whether to pay off bills or buy a truck, etc. These good-intentioned actions were the opposite of what Josh needed as they discouraged responsibility and accountability and fueled the addiction. This was over seven years ago. We begged him to go to a long-term drug rehab program. Without help, without getting healthy, it was impossible for him to have a relationship with his family, with a girlfriend or most importantly with God. He rejected this option. Josh chose to leave Pennsylvania not long after. During the next three plus years, I did not hear from him. I was not sure where he was and if he was even still alive.

I prayed and prayed for him as he was always on my heart and mind. I was still believing that he was in God's hands.

Then one July morning, I was watching Jack's softball game with a very good friend, Jean, who knew and loved Josh from childhood. All of a sudden, my phone rang and incredibly—it was Josh! God had answered my prayers and was true to His word, "I'll catch him." Jean and I both sat there with tears in our eyes. Tears of relief and happiness. Josh had called to ask for help. He sounded very depleted and humbled. He had been living out of his car. Would Pastor Jim help get him into a program? I gave him Pastor's phone number.

In the meantime, I encouraged Josh to seek medical attention there in North Carolina. Shortly thereafter, Pastor Jim did help Josh get into a program in Connecticut. There I saw how God took care of Josh in every way. He received needed hernia surgery. He saw a counselor regularly. He lived in a group home where they conducted classes to identify issues, triggers, etc. and he also helped with Bible studies. He graduated from the program and moved back to North Carolina.

I've heard some people ask, "Why doesn't he just choose to stop using?" I've learned that sobriety is much harder than just saying I want to change. The drug use is to cover up pain if even for a few minutes. Sobriety is about uncovering the root causes of that pain and seeking God's help to heal the wounds and pain from the past.

Today, I feel that I can finally breathe a sigh of relief after so many years of holding my breath and wondering if we would ever get to the root of Josh's problems. Exhale—breath out!

Not that as his mother I have any control of the desired outcome, but I can see where Josh is facing his problems, seeking solutions, seeking God and a healthy, productive life. After so many years of watching my son struggle and vacillate between sobriety and addiction, I truly believe that he has received the care and support he needed. And *he* has been driving the process. In the end, we cannot change another. They must be willing to seek help to change and I am so very thankful that Josh is. Just as importantly, we must also be willing to change our own enabling behavior which I am.

How do I know this time is different? Well it *is* different. How? I believe that he has faced his issues and identified the root of his pain. I am so thankful and so proud of how Josh is rebuilding his life. In so many ways, he has humbled himself—working at menial jobs, taking the bus as transportation. He is willing to take responsibility, pay his fines. And God is honoring his efforts.

After applying for many jobs, he was recently hired as part of a lawn mowing crew owned by a very successful businessman. Josh describes him as very kind and very willing to teach Josh how to run a business, give appropriate estimates, etc.

Josh is certified and very skilled in hardscaping[17]. I believe that God has now opened up opportunities for him to use those skills and perform the work that he loves. His boss is providing a truck for his use and is teaching Josh how to be a businessman not just a laborer.

In these last few years, he has not asked me for *anything*—except prayer and encouragement which I am so happy to provide. I have forced myself to sit back and not get in God's way. I have watched as each week God has miraculously opened another door.

Waiting is one of the hardest things to do. We live in a time of instant gratification. Most of us, including myself, prefer when we are in control. Right? But when we have no human options, I've learned that I must trust that God is still working—even if I don't see it—even if it takes years.

It is in the waiting that faith is built. It is in those times of holding our breath that trust is built. Exhale! Breathe in the peace, comfort, and strength that only the Lord can provide. As Josh would say, "God's light shines brightest after the darkness." And it is shining bright!

Jack and I recently visited Josh in North Carolina a couple of times. It was so wonderful to see him and hug him! He and I talk or text at least once a week. He is the person God made him to be—sweet, kind, thoughtful, appreciative, and hard working.

I want to encourage other mothers, fathers and families who might have children who seem to be "falling." God loves your child, too.

---

[17] The man-made features used in landscape architecture, e.g., paths, walls or walks.

Keep praying. Stay encouraged. God's promises are greater than your circumstances!

Life Lesson

I have learned to trust God in not only <u>what</u> He will do (catch him) but also in <u>how</u> He will do it. I used to decide on a particular way in which God should work (as if He needed my help)—send him to this program in South Carolina, or send him to that program in Connecticut. Only God knows what Josh needs. God has been opening one door after another for Josh (without my help) and in the process Josh has seen that his Heavenly Father loves him too.

> *Wait on the Lord; Be of good courage,*
> *And He shall strengthen your heart;*
> *Wait, I say, on the Lord!*
> Psalm 27:14

After Note

While Josh was still in Connecticut and right after he had successfully completed the program there, I went on a day trip with Pastor Jim to visit him. It had now been twenty plus years since Josh had given me his study Bible and I decided it was time to gift it back to him. The following is the note I wrote on the inside cover:

~~~~~~

Dear Josh,

This is your Mount Zion School of Ministry Bible. You gave it to me, and I am so grateful. This Bible convinced me to believe in the Bible and all that it says.

As you read it, I pray that the Holy Spirit will encourage and inspire you to share powerful and courageous messages.

Although your name imprint on the cover has faded, I pray that the name of Jesus never fades from your heart.

Love always,

Mom

IN SEARCH OF . . .
A DIAGNOSIS

Back in 2005, I had surgery on my right foot. I never understood how one of my two feet could have a problem. Both feet had always been together. Never once had one gone out without the other! After the surgery, the right foot was always numb. I questioned whether a nerve was injured during the surgery. But then, to my surprise, I noticed the left foot also becoming numb. No surgery on that one. What could be happening?

Around the same time, I was having balance issues causing falls and sprains. One night as I left church and walked to my car, one of our church members, stopped me and asked, "Pastor Bev, are you alright?" I think they may have thought I was drunk as I was staggering! Something was definitely not right.

Sometimes the most frustrating part of a disease is determining the correct diagnosis. In 2011, a local neurologist diagnosed that I had a "neuropathy"—no other information or solution offered. I was next misdiagnosed by another neurologist at a renowned Pennsylvania hospital as having "a back problem." Before you start experiencing the same frustration I did, I'll cut right to it. It was *not* a back problem.

At the next visit to the local neurologist, I met with his Nurse Practitioner. (By the way, are these not the most wonderful, caring, and knowledgeable people?) I wanted an opinion on my workout plan for the gym. I explained that I was doing two sets of one exercise, working up to three sets, three sets of another working up to . . . I also used the elliptical machine for half an hour, but I was so weak afterwards that I could hardly walk to my car.

With a look of disbelief on her face, she ordered me to sit there and stay put. She quickly returned with the head of their Physical Therapy (PT) Department. These two women spent the next fifteen minutes mentally "slapping me from one side of my head to the other." "Don't you understand? You have a disease! You cannot be working *up* to anything. You have Charcot-Marie-Tooth[18] (CMT) disease!" Definitely a strange name—having no need for a dentist. It was actually named after the three doctors who discovered it. They further explained, "There is a CMT Association—look online. This is a progressive disease. Yes, you should exercise but too much can cause further damage."

I left the office in shock, went to my car and cried. Then I went to McDonald's for a real "pity party" and decided right then and there—enough of the pitying. I prayed that God would give me the strength to endure and went about my day and my life.

Jack and I began visiting CMT support groups which provided a wealth of information. Through them I learned of Dr. Steven Scherer of the University of Pennsylvania, a neurologist who had spent his entire career on CMT research. I felt very blessed to be under the care of one of the top CMT neurologists in the world! Although there is no cure for CMT currently, there is much research underway. It was so encouraging to be seen by a doctor who totally understood what I was experiencing. There were also CMT Patient Conferences with renowned speakers and helpful information. I learned the good news was that CMT only affects the arms and legs and that it is not fatal.

---

[18] CMT is a hereditary motor and sensory neuropathy of the peripheral nervous system characterized by progressive loss of muscle tissue and touch sensation.

I was referred to a wonderful orthotist who designed custom leg braces for me. Wow! What a difference. As I practiced the first time I put them on, I felt as if I could strut down a runway. Before we left the University of Penn, I visited the rest room before our long ride home. I was feeling so optimistic—until I tried to stand up. It seems that the same ridged graphite braces that enabled me to stand, also prevented me from standing up! Help—I sat down and I can't get up! Eventually, I did but I also required physical therapy to learn how to properly function.

While at PT, the therapist asked me if I would mind talking to a young teenage girl who was quite depressed. She was being fitted for the same type of leg braces that I had. I was so happy that I could be an encouragement. After a brief talk, I showed her my runway strut and had her laughing. There are so many worse things to have to cope with than CMT. I am so thankful for my leg braces in that they enable me to stand and walk. I could still preach and walk to my car—like a sober person!

Our first great granddaughter, Kinsley, always seemed fascinated by my braces. When she was just starting to walk, I would make light of my braces by knocking on them and asking, "Is anyone home?" She would giggle. Recently, she turned three years old, and she very seriously asked, "Nana, why must you wear those braces?" Oh boy, how was I going to translate my answer into three-year-old language? First, I asked her if we could both feel her leg calf muscle—"See how strong it is?" Then, I took off one of my braces and invited her to feel my calf muscle. I said, "Yikes—it feels all squishy like a jellyfish, right?" (My leg muscles are quite atrophied.) I assured her that my muscles did not hurt but the saddest expression came onto this child's precious little face. Without any words, her face was saying, "Why does my Nana have to have this?" Only God holds the answer to that question.

Life Lesson

We never know what trials will come our way. We can't control whether we contract a disease, but we can control how we will react—we can have an ongoing pity party or choose to keep on going as best we can—with God's help. I have learned so much about weakness and strength. The apostle Paul captures it so well in the scripture below.

> *And He said to me, "My grace is sufficient for you,*
> *for My strength is made perfect in weakness."*
> *Therefore most gladly I will rather boast in my infirmities,*
> *that the power of Christ may rest upon me.*
> 2 Corinthians 12:9

JUST TOO MUCH

I loved my role as Associate Pastor. Serving our congregation and supporting Pastor Jim and was so fulfilling. I really found my purpose. It was a lot of work, but also so much fun. And very freeing from the corporate life of structure and layers of decision making—*and* we could pray before a meeting. What a difference!

Since my CMT diagnosis in 2012, I had been able to continue as the Associate Pastor. I could not have done this without the support of my husband and my Pastor.

My husband, Jack, has always been an active partner in our marriage doing many of the household chores even before my CMT. He loves grocery shopping. I don't. He jokes that this was one of the reasons I married him. He's always been very hands-on with the children and grandchildren. He's been my biggest advocate—in whichever path I was led down—college, ministry, art, CMT, or writing.

After we retired from our corporate lives, he had dreams of RVing around the country, but ministry and pastoring took precedence. Although I do think he liked being called "the Pastor's wife." At the end of 2015, several events precipitated some changes.

I shared with you how City Limits has several outreaches a year. With normal, healthy legs, it could be exhausting but that year I reached my limit during our Christmas Tree Outreach. There were hundreds of people attending and many City Limits leaders. I was trying to help out everywhere—flitting from one area to another. That night, I could barely drive myself home and walked into the house where I just collapsed and broke down. It was *just too much* for me physically. Up to now, I always focused on what I *could* do. Now the reality struck me of what I *couldn't* do—fulfill the role of Associate Pastor. Outreaches were such a big part of our ministry and I felt very inadequate. I was heartbroken. I met with Pastor Jim and Deborah and shared my intention to retire from my role. I had no intention of leaving the church. *You cannot retire from relationships!* The truth was it was also time to raise up some younger ministers. I held off telling Jack of my retirement plans which leads us to . . .

The second pivotal event—Jack was turning seventy-years old that year. I felt it was time to devote time to us. We planned a special anniversary trip to Cape May, New Jersey. This is where we spent our honeymoon, thirty years prior and this is where I planned to surprise him.

For his anniversary gift, I gave him a poem (see the next page) to announce that I was retiring from the role of Associate Pastor. He was shocked, speechless. I think he said something like he would more likely believe I would leave him before I would leave the ministry!

Through the Years - Thirty Official Years of Marriage -
Jack and Bev Fekula
December 13, 1985 - December 13, 2015

Through the years
We've shared laughs and tears.

Four Children
Eight Grandchildren
Gave us many reasons to grin.

Much faith and many prayers
Have soothed our hearts
and calmed our cares.

What a great husband you are
and especially my shopping super star!

You are always there with a hug and a kiss
any opportunities for these I would not miss.

In retirement, I'm so sorry
I've been a little tardy.

Instead of RVing on the road
We've been detoured into ministry mode.

Pastor Bev and Pastor's Wife
Has really given us quite a life!

I love you more today than then
and feel my ways I should finally mend.

I've been retired and refired
but now I'm just plain old tired.

You've been so patient, so kind
and what's really on my mind
Is making time for just us two
which seems to me much overdue.

We prayed about a new Associate Pastor and within a year, a ministry credentialed woman started to attend our services. She was praying about being an Associate Pastor! Sometimes I think situations are about me. They rarely are. She filled the role and also recommended her friend as the Children's Pastor. Our church was doubly blessed. This would not have happened if I hadn't "retired."

Many pastors upon receiving such retirement news would move on and work with the new Associate—not Pastor Jim. He continued to include me in special meetings and appreciated my input. Jack always says that I'm "actively retired." One day, we were in the middle of a meeting when I noticed new church business cards in the middle of the conference room table. The previous cards simply had the church information and Pastor Jim's and my name on. I was expecting to see the new pastors' names which were there but then I looked at the top of the list:

Pastor Jim Rivera - Lead Pastor
Pastor Bev Fekula - Executive Pastor

What—Executive Pastor?? I just retired and it looks like I got a promotion[19]! How sweet and thoughtful. Thank you, Pastor Jim. I still occasionally teach and preach but will never retire from all the special relationships I formed—from all the people I love.

---

[19] For the record, the church can only afford to pay Pastor Jim and not with much regularity.

Life Lesson

God still sees our value even if we don't. He will use amazing people to help us see ourselves through His eyes.

> *A new commandment I give to you,*
> *that you love one another;*
> *as I have loved you,*
> *that you also love one another.*
> John 13:34

WHY GOD?

I have to admit that after a year or so, I was really missing my old pastoring role. One morning during my prayers I wondered why God called me into ministry so late in my life, only to have me disabled by Charcot-Marie-Tooth (CMT) disease just a few years after becoming ordained. I asked, "Why God?" Not "why me" in a "pity party" way, but in a "there must be a greater purpose" way. The better question was, "What do you want me to do because of this disease"? I had been focusing on me not on God's purpose. I needed to search for the answer.

As I prayed, a person came to mind—Joni Eareckson Tada. I had heard her for the first time on a radio show years before. She shared how she and her husband went to Jerusalem and there she was in her wheelchair at the pool of Bethesda[20]. She prayed, "Thank You God for healing me." Now I'm driving and thinking to myself, "Didn't she just say that she was in a wheelchair?" She went on to explain that God had chosen not to heal her physically, but He had healed her emotionally and spiritually. WOW! What a spiritual soul changer!

Why was Joni in a wheelchair? In 1967, at seventeen years of age, Joni dove into shallow water that left her a quadriplegic—dramatically

---

[20] Gospel of John 5:2-6

changing her life. In the early years of her disability, she would pray to Jesus for physical healing as she had read about in the Bible. Amazingly, over the years her disability brought thousands of people to know the love of God and to bring respect and dignity to the disabled. She was on the National Council on Disability and attended the signing of the Americans with Disabilities Act in 1990.

In 2000, she began the "Wheels for the World" ministry where her team not only brought wheelchairs but the love of God and salvation to so many—100,000 worldwide. I could go on and on . . . To learn more about Joni's story, see the joniandfriends.org website.

So, you can see why I sought out Joni and her ministry. While reading her website, I noticed an extensive Certificate Program that was being offered called, "Beyond Suffering." The course description explained how "people with disabilities are one of the world's most under-represented groups." The goal was to prepare leaders in various fields, including ministers, to address this issue. What a learning experience!

The program was more intensive than any of the Master level courses I had attended. In addition to reading the textbook, there were weekly assignments, discussion boards, videos, lectures, papers written from experts in many different fields and—writing project and ministry papers. It was so fascinating and informative to talk with fellow students from around the world—for example, to hear what it's like to get on the Tube (subway) in London in a wheelchair.

At first, I thought that God was leading me to this course for me personally—perhaps to prepare me to minister at nursing homes or rehabilitation centers. But after just two weeks, I clearly saw how God wanted to start a disability ministry at my church, City Limits. The course revealed how many disabled people, or their children feel unwelcome in churches. Every human being has value and contributes to the church body. I thought about Robbie, a severely mentally disabled young man who comes to our church each Sunday. He is unable to speak but he smiles broadly while playing along with the worship music on his tambourine. What if the sweetest sound Jesus heard on Sunday mornings was Robbie's joyful tambourine? How many people are there that don't attend church, don't know that God loves them—just as they are.

God gives clear instructions to the church in Luke 14:21. Joni and Friends is answering that call, "invite the poor, the crippled, the lame, the blind and you will be blessed...make them come in so my house will be full." Jesus was not making a suggestion but a mandate—go quickly; compel them to come.

"Why God?" "Why does my Nana have to wear those braces?"

I believe that God was finally answering our questions. God does have a greater purpose. He does have a reason for my disability.

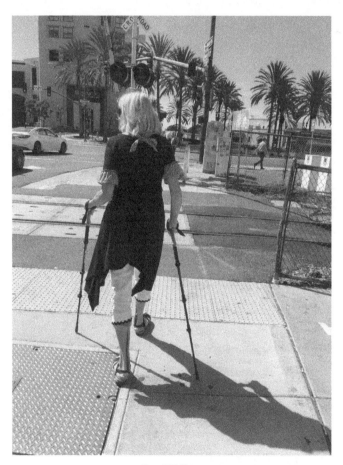

Bev Walking

Life Lesson

So many times when we experience a trial, sickness, disease, heartbreak, grief, our focus is inward—on how this is affecting us. I've learned that it is rarely about me.

> *But those who wait on the Lord*
> *Shall renew their strength;*
> *They shall mount up with wings like eagles,*
> *They shall run and not be weary,*
> *They shall walk and not faint.*
> Isaiah 40:31

THE DISABILITY MINISTRY

The *Beyond Suffering* course teaches that "without clear statements of belief, the church itself is in danger of becoming a disabled body"—a frightening thought! With renewed purpose and spiritual enthusiasm, I met with Pastor Jim and his Associate and shared all that I learned and where I felt God was leading us—toward a Disability Ministry. We needed to be deliberate—pray and plan. We had some work to do before we could have a "Luke 14" dinner as God instructed to the church in Luke 14:21—"invite the poor, the crippled, the lame, the blind and you will be blessed."

I reached out to our community and found an awesome partner in the Lehigh Valley Center for Independent Living (CIL). They evaluated our building and provided a seventy-two page recommendations report—free! Basically, we needed a handicap ramp into our one hundred- and sixty-year-old church and modifications to our first floor bathroom.

One Sunday, I preached a "Luke 14" message explaining how God wants us to be welcoming and reach out to the disabled. I shared the vision and engaged the congregation. Instead of an altar call, I asked for a donation/pledge call. One faithful person pledged a dollar a week until we reach our goal! So sweet! Our church is very financially challenged.

Only Pastor Jim gets paid (occasionally), so we knew this would be a leap of faith. So far, we have raised $16,756.97. A huge miracle!

Although the COVID 19 virus stalled the installation of the handicap ramp, I firmly believed that if God wants this ministry, it *will* happen.

We were also led to an engineer who created a blueprint with all the design specifications that were needed for the work permits. This also was a donation.

On May 13, 2021, our cement handicap ramp was poured! (See photos at the end of the chapter.) I thank and praise God! There is still much physical work to be done. We also had to create a new side door as the ramp entrance. In the meantime, we are investigating other ways we could support the community, such as, support groups for autism and serving the deaf and hard of hearing community with "signing" at our services.

I am so humbled that God answered my prayer of "Why God?" I believe He also wants you to know that His purpose for you will be fulfilled!

Life Lesson

Through my CMT[21] disease, God gave me an empathy and a heart for all those with disabilities. He also enabled me to see that I still have value even with my atrophied legs. There is more to life than limbs!

> *And we know that all things work together for good*
> *to those who love God,*
> *to those who are the called*
> *according to His purpose.*
> Romans 8:28

---

[21] Charcot-Marie-Tooth Disease

Bev Helping with Ramp

Deborah Beautifying Area—See Ramp in Background

Pastor Jim Power Washing

Ramp to Side Door

IN SEARCH OF . . .
GOD'S PATH

As I wrote this book, I realized a beautiful pattern in my life. At so many pivotal decision points, the decision path was already laid before me with the doors wide open. I just needed to walk through those doors.

My mother always said, "Everything happens for a reason." Maybe you heard that from someone, too. In retrospect, we can see the reasons why doors are laid open and awaiting our passing through.

Looking forward as a child or as a teenager you wonder what your life will hold. You never really think that there will be disappointments, hurts and sorrows. But there is such value in looking backwards as an adult and seeing how God uses *everything* for our good and for His purpose.

Let me share some examples:

Single Mom	I absolutely never considered divorce.
Corporate Career	I had planned on being a stay-at-home mom.
College	I never desired to go to college.
Ministry	I never aspired to be a minister or a pastor.
Art	I definitely never thought of myself as an artist.
Disability Ministry	I certainly never anticipated such a disease as CMT.
Writing	I never thought of myself as an author.

Expanding on the previous examples:

Single Mom	*I absolutely never considered divorce.* Here I had to walk out of one door and into another. None of the remaining examples would have happened if I had not taken those walks.
Corporate Career	*I had planned on being a stay-at-home mom.* This opened the door to a wonderful new life—a loving husband, two great step-children and two college degrees.
College	*I never desired to go to college.* At thirty-three, I realized the value of college and the application of the learning to my corporate position. This opened the door to international travel and an appreciation of new cultures that were valuable in ministry at our multi-cultural church.
Ministry	*I never aspired to be a minister or a pastor.* As I drew closer in my relationship with God, He opened the doors of opportunities to serve Him.

Art	*I definitely never thought of myself as an artist.* This could still be debated! However, I wouldn't be a "want-to-be" artist if the door to art classes wasn't offered and opened.
Disability Ministry	*I certainly never anticipated such a disease as CMT.* I must admit that as I write this, it brings tears to my eyes. Isn't it peculiar that what might be considered one of the tragedies of my life was the very thing that God has used the most?
Writing	*I never thought of myself as an author.* One of my "Tiki Hut" friends, Allen, an author himself, so encouraged me to write this book. He knocked on this writing door so loudly by emailing me each week asking where the next chapter was. I truly thank him for the motivation. If you are reading this book, it means that the writing door sprung open wide!

The greatest pleasure is when you realize that you did walk through many of the doors that God opened for you. I personally wonder if there were doors I was meant to walk through and didn't. How about you?

Why don't we walk through open doors? Sometimes we are unsure what lies on the other side, or we do know and it's the scariest thing we've ever considered. Perhaps we feel unqualified, insecure, or uneducated. Please trust me that if God is opening a door for you, He will equip you. He will strengthen you and He will be your encourager.

You do not have to be a minister, a pastor or for that matter an artist, writer or disabled. God has special doors designated just for you. Only *you*. Please be sensitive to the doors that lay open in your life.

May God bless you and provide you with many doors.

> *5 Trust in the Lord with all your heart,*
> *And lean not on your own understanding;*
>
> *6 In all your ways acknowledge Him,*
> *And He shall direct your paths.*
> Proverbs 3:5-6

EPILOGUE

Closing Encouragements from Life Lessons

- Pray and ask God to guide your path. Then walk through the doorways.
- Continue to learn. It will open your eyes and heart to new experiences and new people.
- Be prepared to serve others. It is impossible to serve others without blessings being returned to you.
- Do not be discouraged. Every trial will bring you closer to God—if you allow it.
- Each day, ask if your priorities will bring those you know and those you will meet closer to God.
- When physical limitations or disabilities come (and they will if you live long enough), accept them and focus not on what you can no longer do but on what you can do.
- See people through God's eyes. We all have weaknesses. Look for the strength in others.
- Forgive lavishly.

- Seek eternal life. This life is so short and temporary. Spend your time wisely.
- Love everyone as God loves you!

Always remember—
Jesus didn't die on the cross to make your life *easy*.
Jesus died on the cross to make your life *eternal*—the final door!

May you always have God in your Life, Strength in your Faith, and Joy in your Family!

AFTERWORD

As explained in the Introduction:

> In Key Largo, Florida in our humble little community
> there is a small beach where the aqua blue ocean and
> the white, sun-bleached Adirondack chairs call to those
> who listen. Here, under the Tiki Hut, friends are made,
> acquaintances are renewed, and relationships are built.
> How? By sharing the stories of our lives.

It was there, under the Tiki Hut that I met my friend, Allen
Kacenjar—a former trial lawyer, an elected public official, an avid fly
fisherman and an author.[22] He also happened to be a fishing buddy of
my husband, Jack.

We chatted occasionally and had many stories to share from our
lives. At the end of the season, Allen shared that he thought I had some
really interesting stories—that I should share. Share?! As in a book? I
never ever thought of writing a book.

Soon, along with our spouses, we left Florida and returned to our

---

[22] *INSTANT FLY FISHING . . . JUST ADD WATER*

respective homes in Ohio and Pennsylvania. That's when the emails started arriving. "Where's Chapter One?" Allen was also writing another book and I would retort (please notice my legalese) with, "Where's Your Chapter One?" And on it went—day after day—"Where's Chapter One?"—"Where's Chapter One?" Finally, just to lessen the email traffic flow, I drafted a story. "Good. Where's Chapter Two?" As I started to write a few stories, I noticed a pattern across my life—God was there through it all. Through the sorrows and joys, failures and triumphs; He was guiding me, loving me. Now there was a purpose to it all—to share with others my faith journey. To encourage others who may be experiencing grief, rejection, divorce, addiction and to give them the hope that I found in Jesus.

My sincere gratitude to Allen for without his persistence and encouragement, this book would never have been birthed. Thank you, Allen. May God bless you and your family always.

ABOUT THE AUTHOR

Bev Standing

In seeking a change from the formal "religion" in which she was raised, Bev found a Spirit-filled, Bible-preaching church—City Limits Assembly of God in Allentown, Pa.—a dynamic, multi-cultural church known for its evangelism and community outreaches.

While working full-time at Air Products and Chemicals as a Global Learning Manager, she had the opportunity to teach leadership classes in many countries and coach new leaders. Meanwhile, she began volunteering at church—as a Deaconess, Church Board Member and Spiritual Adviser to women at Lehigh County Prison.

As she heard God calling her into ministry, she studied through

Global University and served as the Associate Pastor, regularly preaching and teaching.

In 2012, she became an ordained minister. She then knew why God gave her those leadership training opportunities—to teach and encourage the ministry team at City Limits. Also, her international travel gave her an appreciation for all people—all races, all cultures—a quality much needed to serve her multi-cultural church.

About eight years ago, she was diagnosed with Charcot-Marie-Tooth (CMT) disease, a neurological muscular disease. Since her mobility is restricted, she stepped down from the Associate Pastor role but continues as the Executive Pastor.

God is also calling her to use her disability to minister to others. City Limits has started a Disability Ministry. They desire to welcome all those who might not know God or who might feel they are not welcome in church.

Bev resides in Orefield, Pa. with Jack, her husband of thirty-six years. They have four children, eight grandchildren and are blessed with two great-granddaughters! They enjoy biking, camping, kayaking, and any activity that involves being with the grandchildren.

CPSIA information can be obtained
at www.ICGtesting.com
Printed in the USA
BVHW041647151122
652010BV00016B/113